Kindness Comes From You

Kindness Comes From You

All that I am is because of the example that I have seen in my mother. To Every Woman who lives her life to ensure that the family is strong, you are beautiful. To the women who impact the lives of children your sacrifice is valued and appreciated. Our Kindness truly comes from you

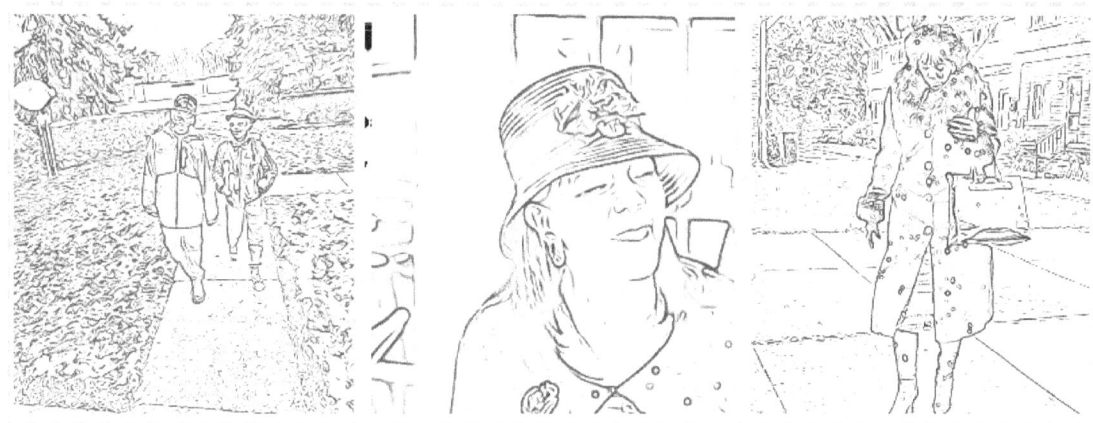

COLORING WITH KINDNESS

#THISISTHEKINDNESS

Richard Patterson III
Kindness Comes From You

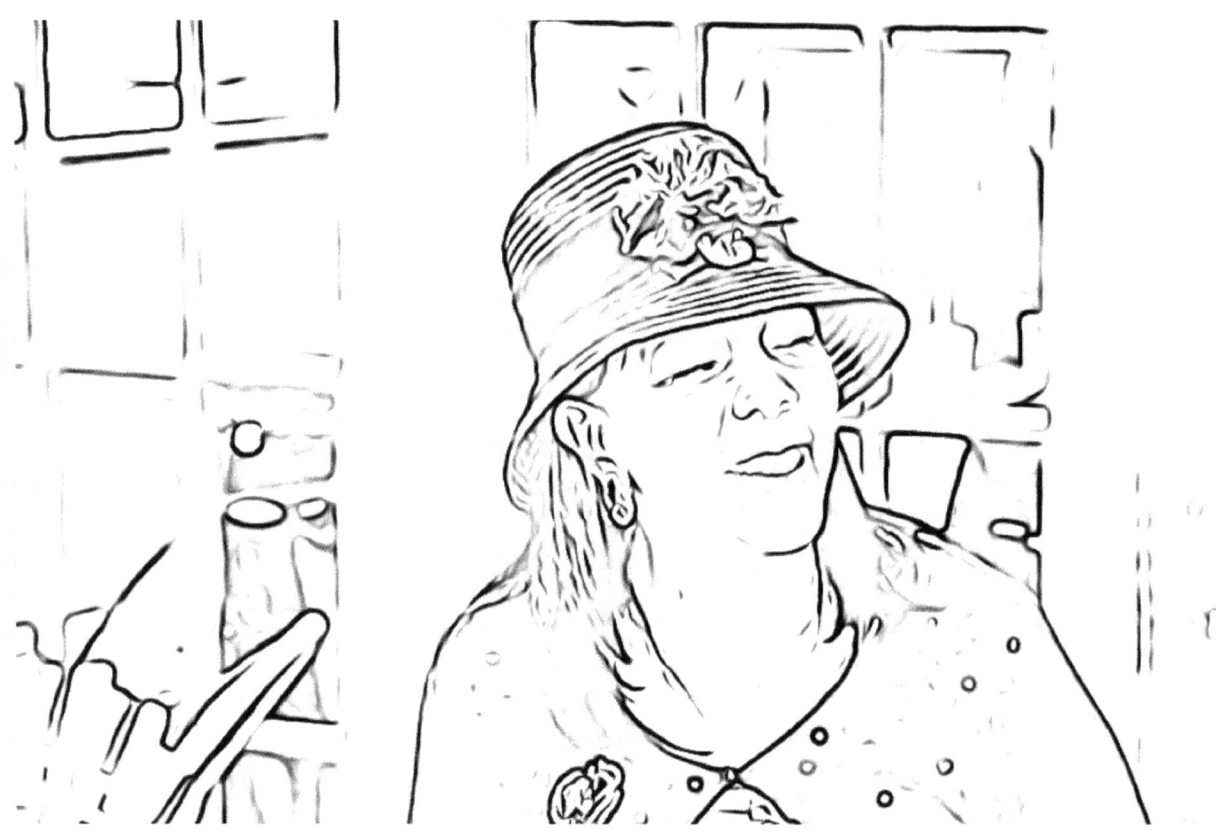

The smile that represents waking up early in the morning, going to work and furthering your education. Your smile represents perseverance and despite having mouths to feed you managed to be kind and productive.

Coloring With Kindness

Richard Patterson III
Kindness Comes From You

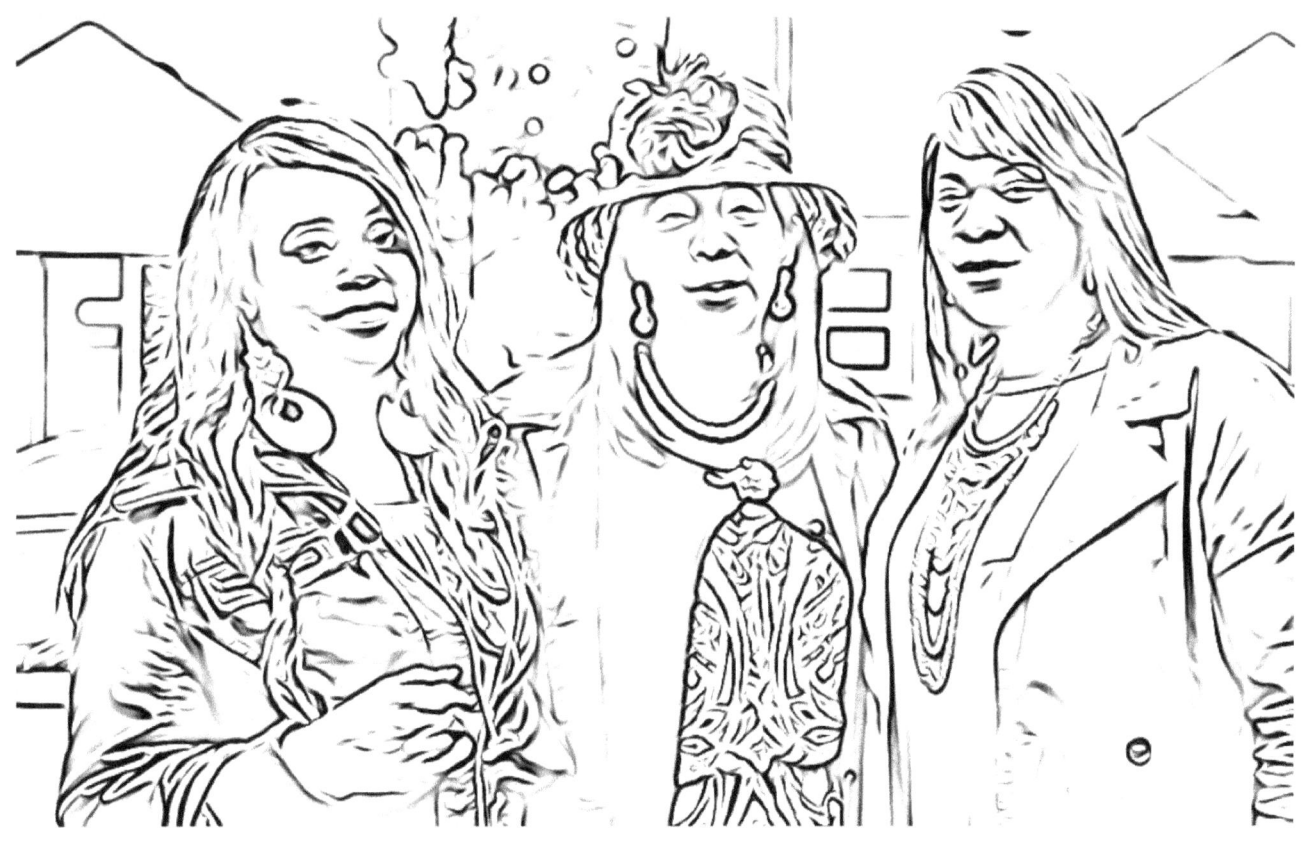

You spent years teaching your daughters, don't just be cute but be productive. Learn how to do hair, make clothes but don't expect a hand out. Your example is your Kindness to the family.

Coloring With Kindness

Richard Patterson III
Kindness Comes From You

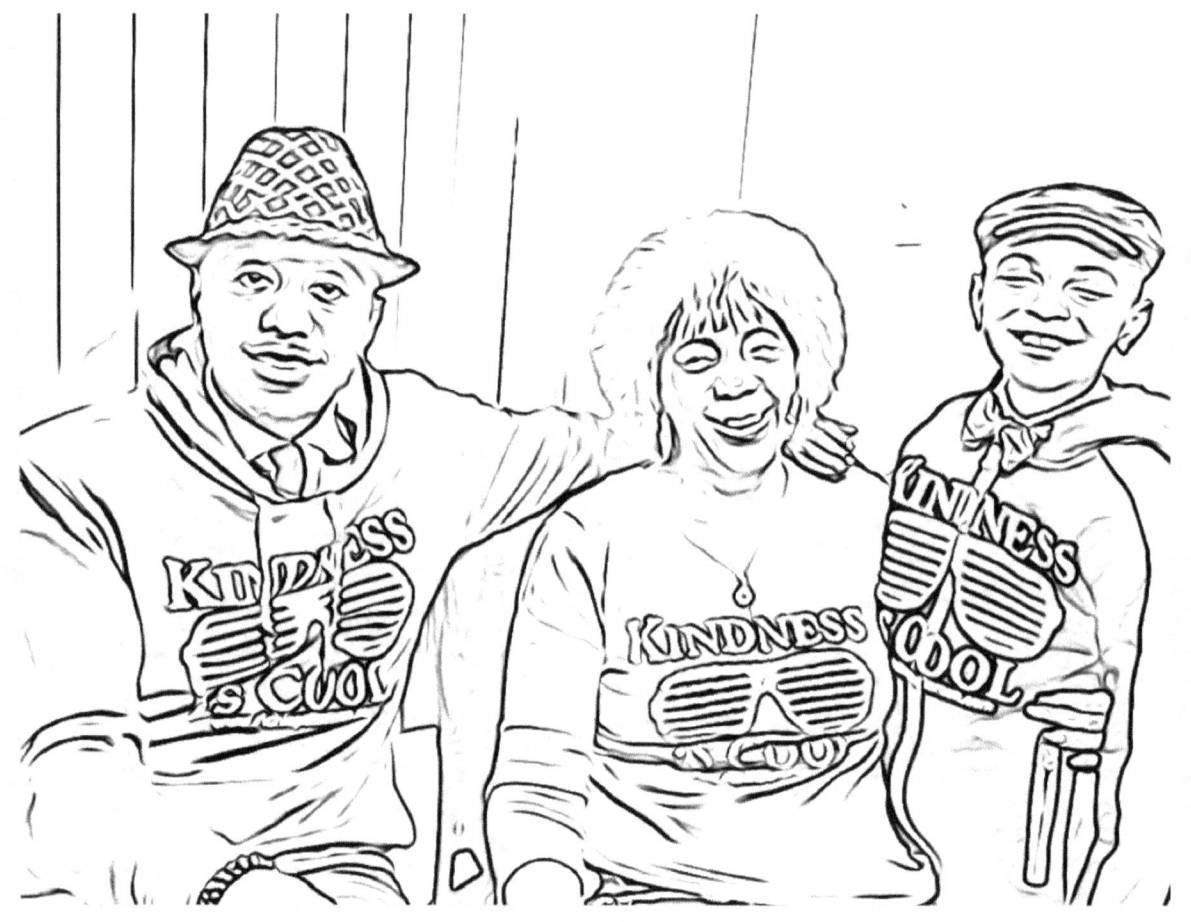

You are respected and many wonder what was your goal in raising your children? You are happy to answer "My Mom and Dad said don't raise them for today alone but raise your children for the future". This is where our Kindness comes from.

Coloring With Kindness

Richard Patterson III
Kindness Comes From You

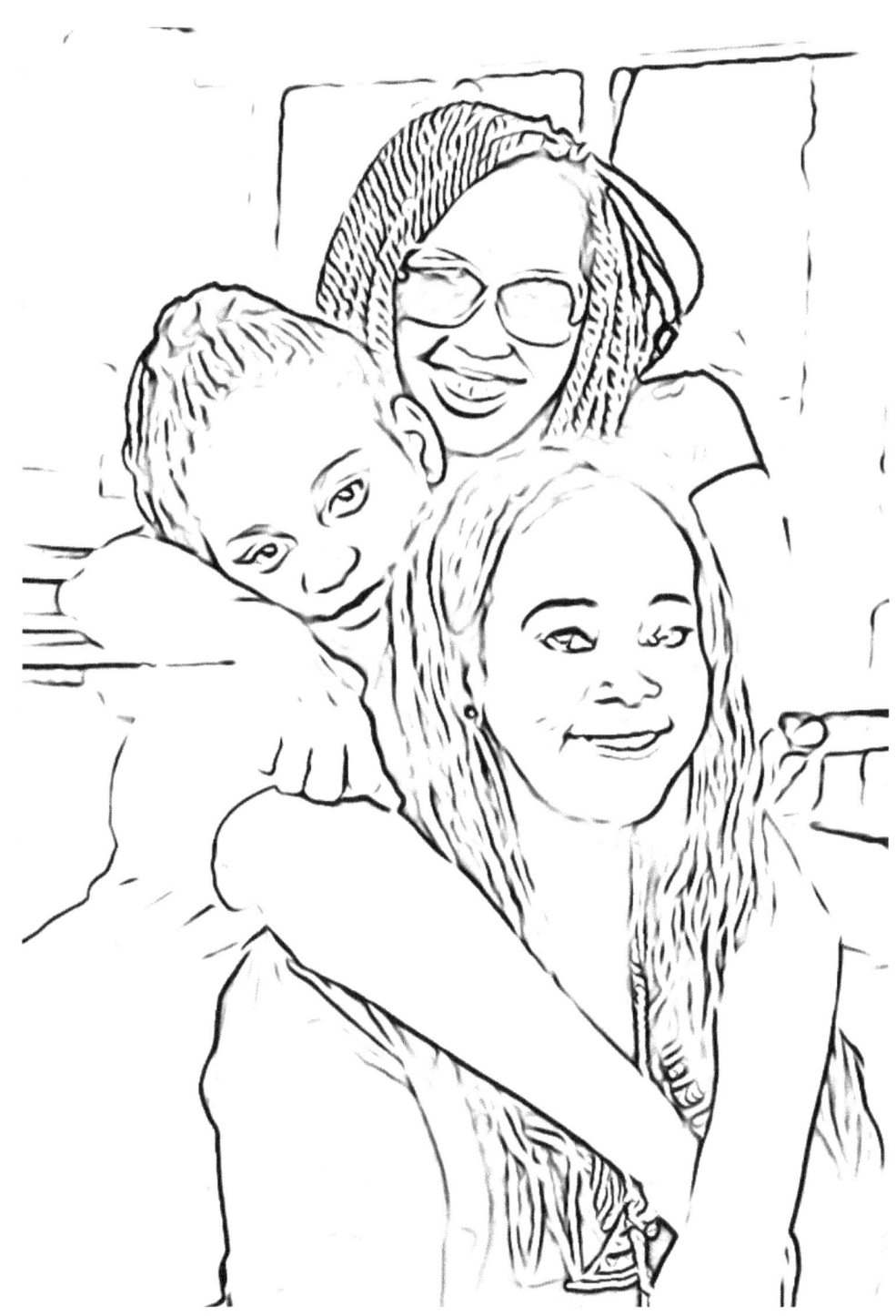

Your example of being engaged with your children has now becomes the living legacy through your children and how they parent.

Coloring With Kindness

Richard Patterson III
Kindness Comes From You

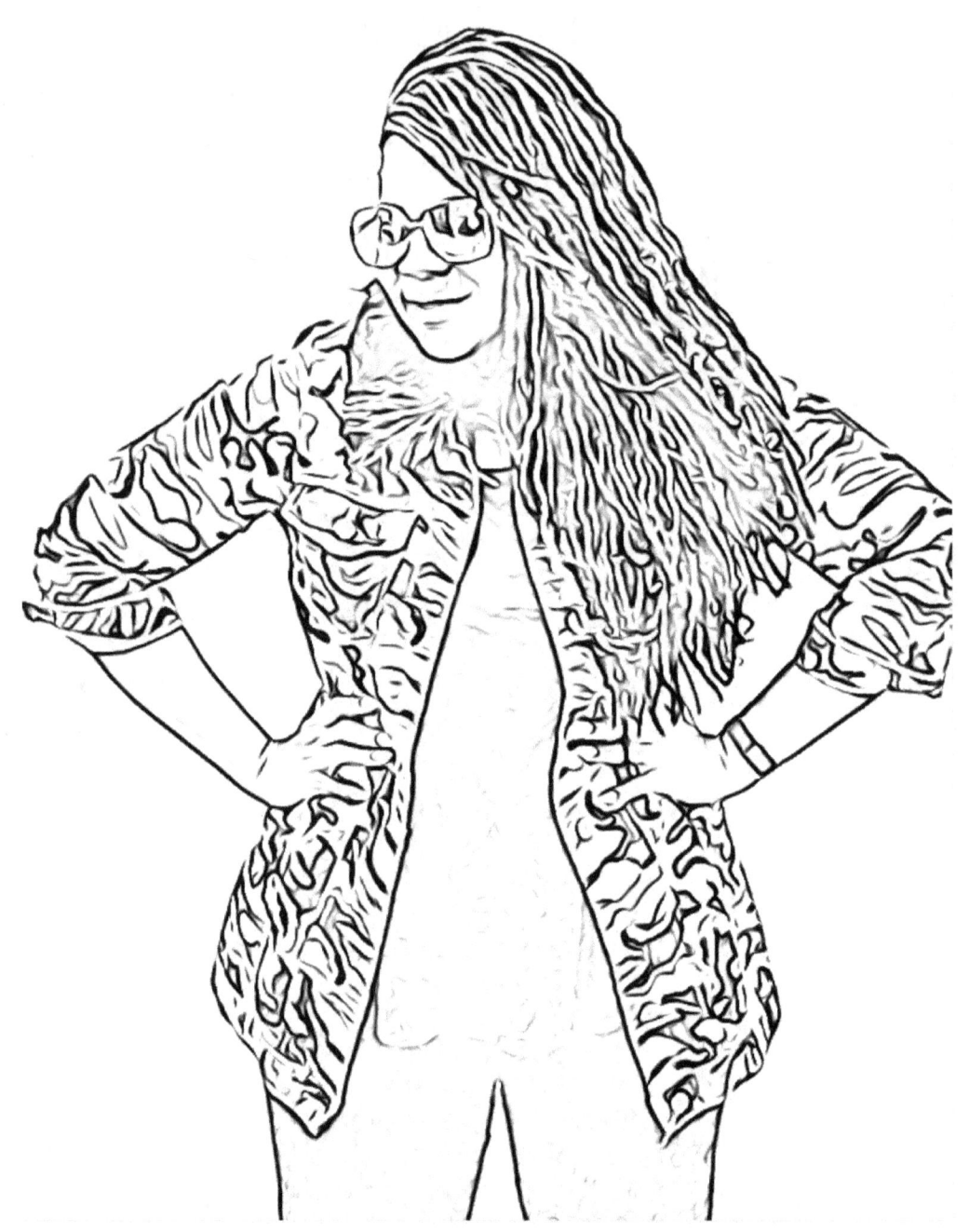

You constantly echoed the importance to master the tasks set before you. Iron your clothes in advance and let finishing give you confidence. Our confidence comes from your Kindness.

Coloring With Kindness

Richard Patterson III
Kindness Comes From You

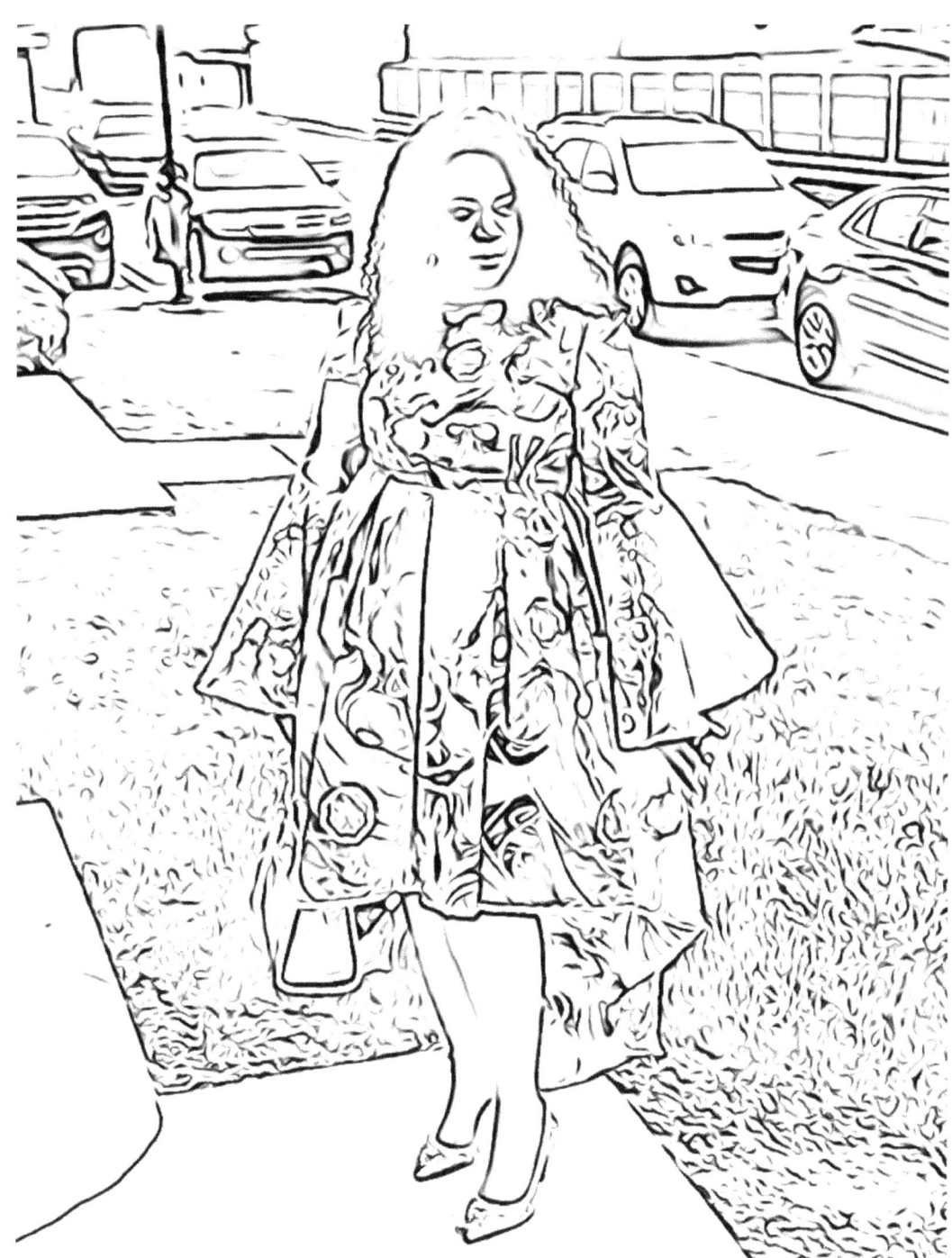

We stand out because you were interested enough to look outside of yourself to consider what would serve us best. Your Kindness created individuality that's second to none.

Coloring With Kindness

Richard Patterson III
Kindness Comes From You

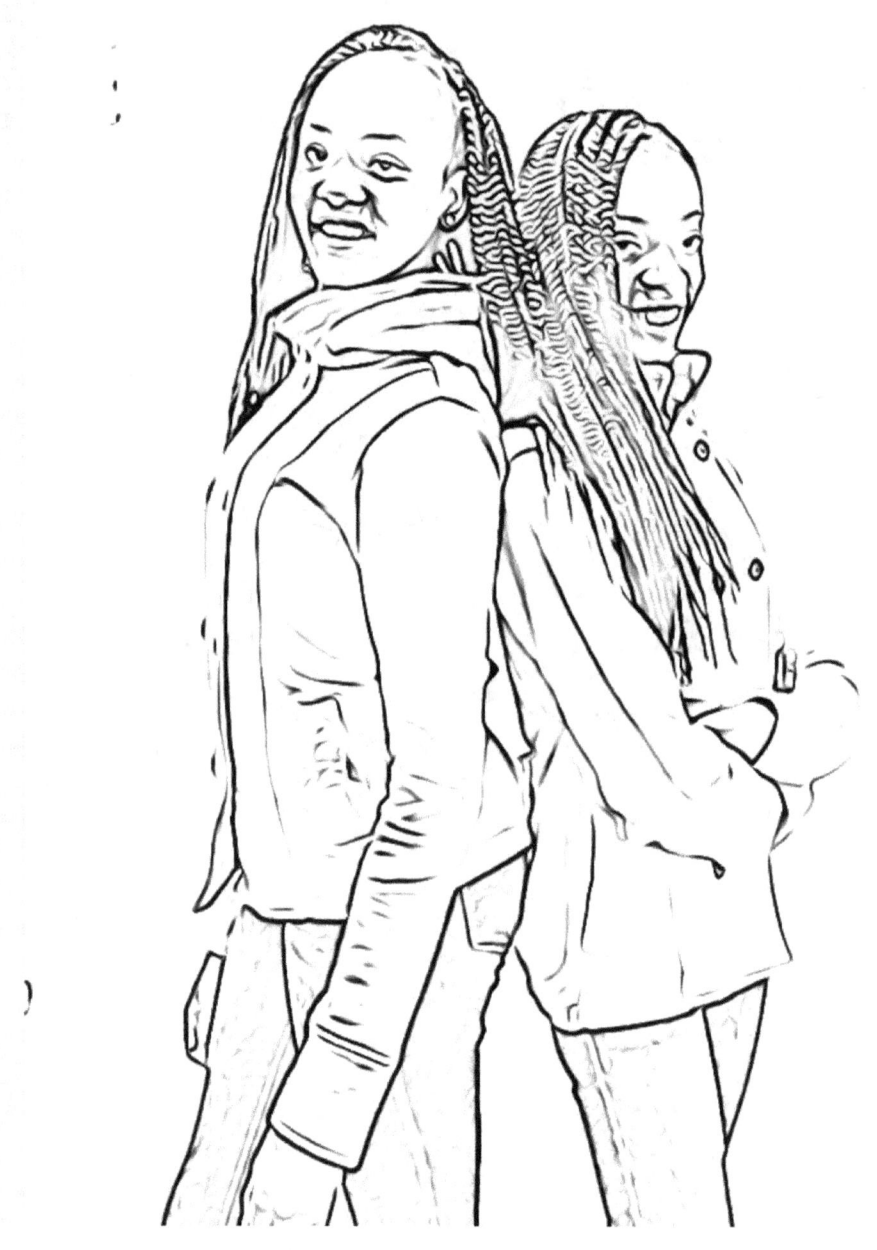

There's another generation embracing who they are. Today you say things like I was tall just like you when I was young but that's our beauty. Your Kindness lives on through your children's (children).

Coloring With Kindness

Richard Patterson III
Kindness Comes From You

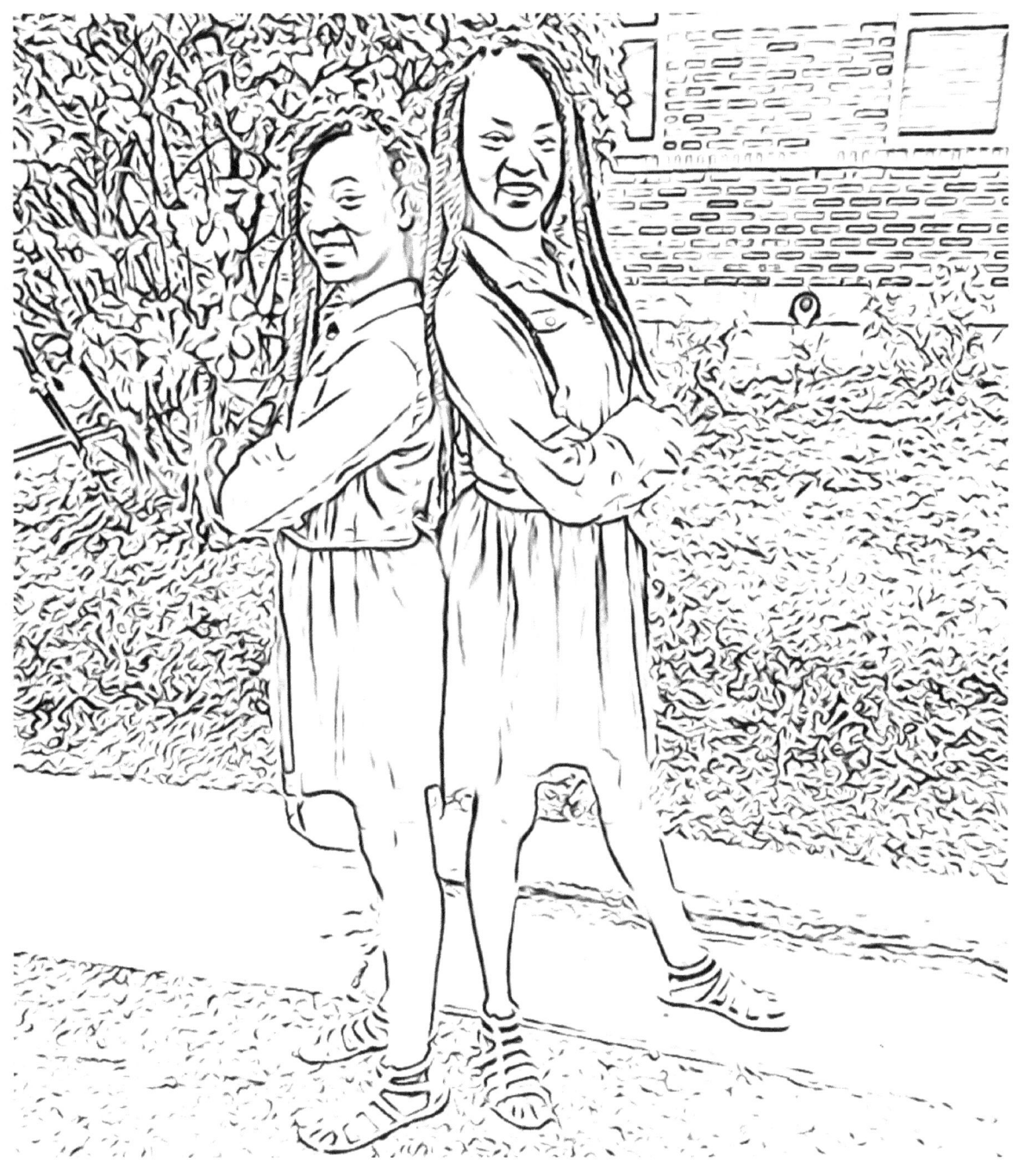

The simple but profound lesson you taught "Always Stick Together". Our Kindness comes from your example.

Coloring With Kindness

Richard Patterson III
Kindness Comes From You

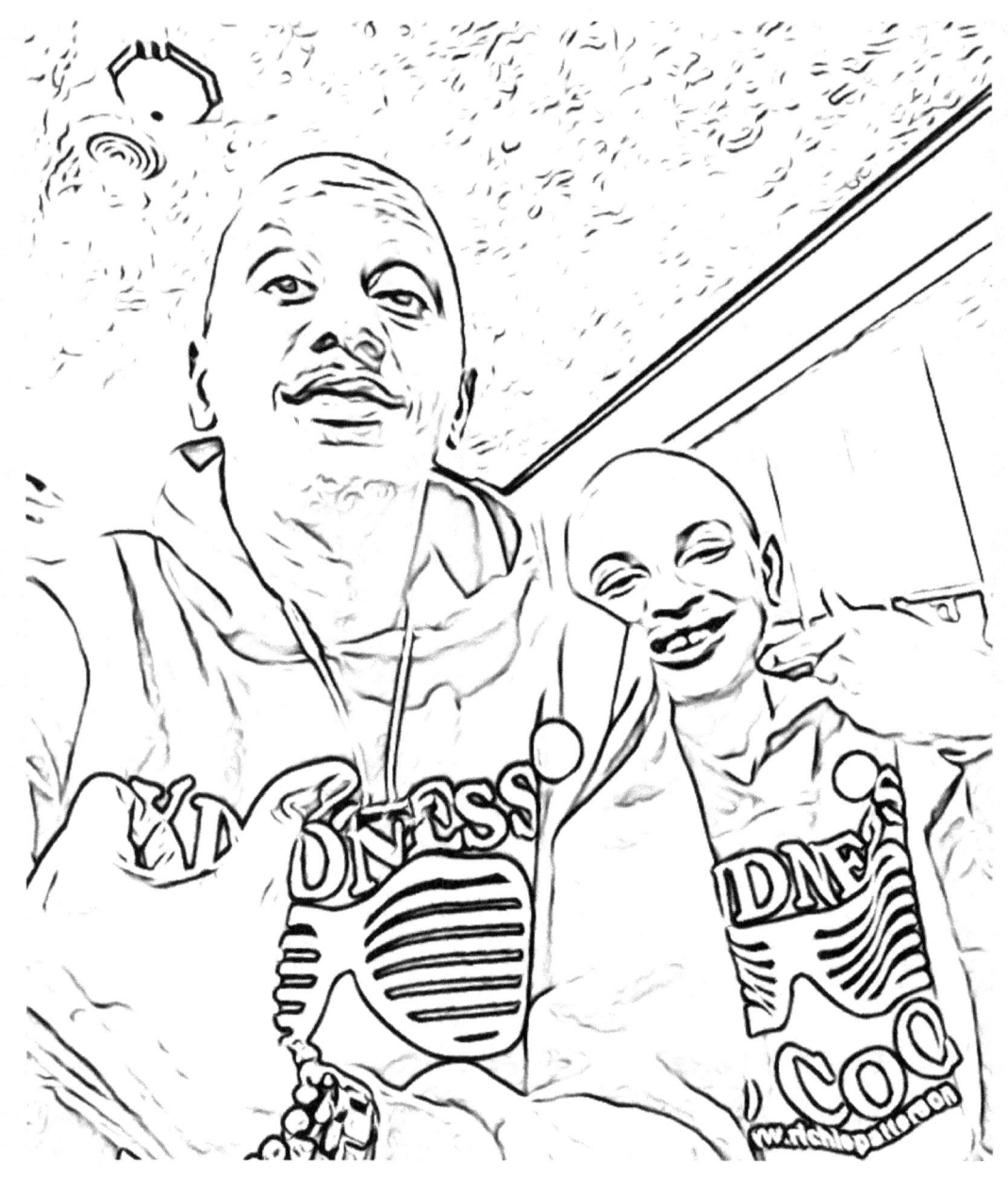

Having no father in the home, you trained sons and exposed them to sources who helped you parent. Now the man who was once a boy is giving the same lessons to his son. Because you are the epitome of Kindness.

Coloring With Kindness

Richard Patterson III
Kindness Comes From You

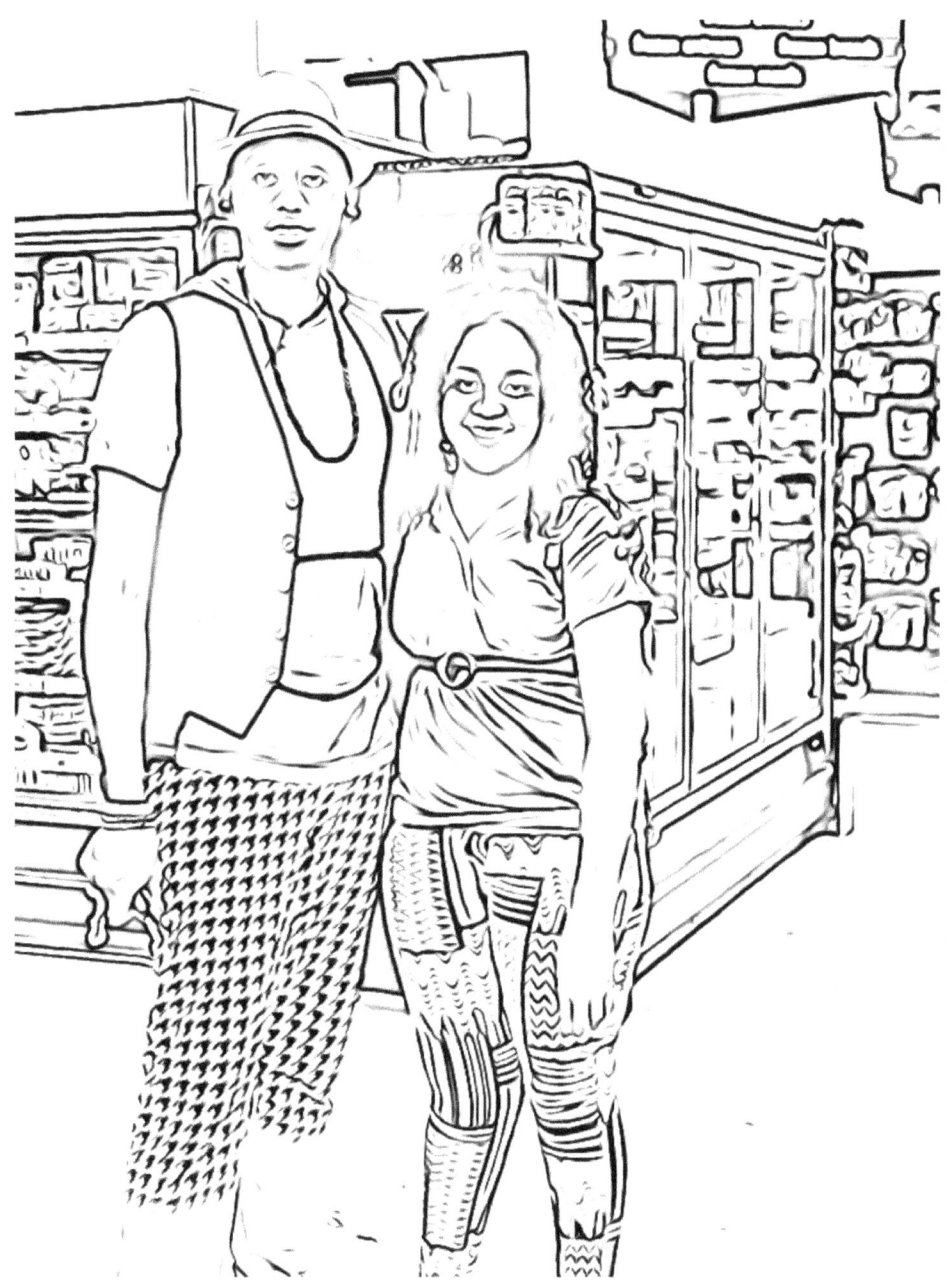

You celebrated the consistency of your father and how he just showed up with love and compassion to see others do well. Your Kindness is why so many men are present and engaged with their children, nieces and nephews.

Coloring With Kindness

Richard Patterson III
Kindness Comes From You

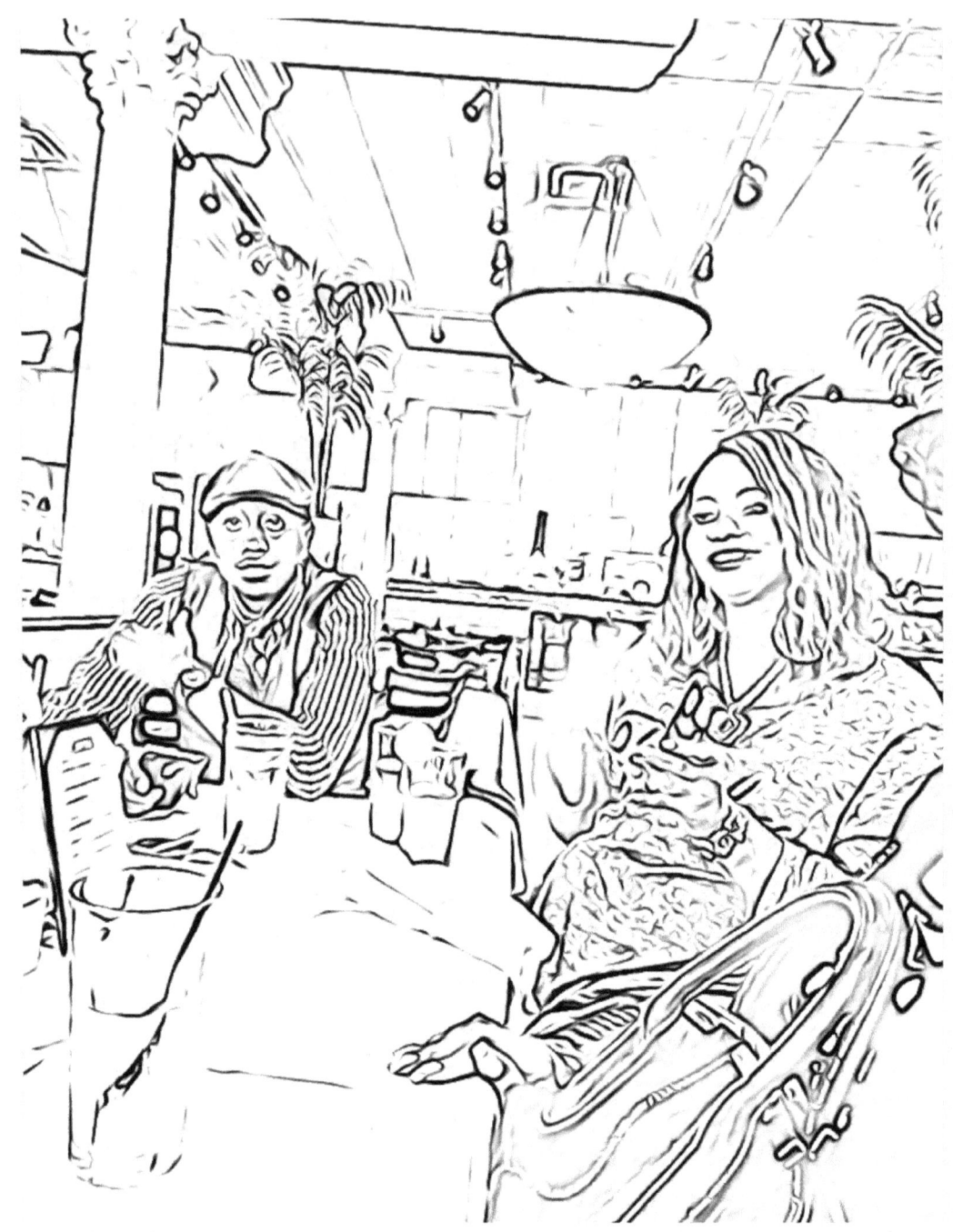

You taught your sons to support your sisters no matter what. Your adult children spend time together because our Kindness comes from you.

Coloring With Kindness

Richard Patterson III
Kindness Comes From You

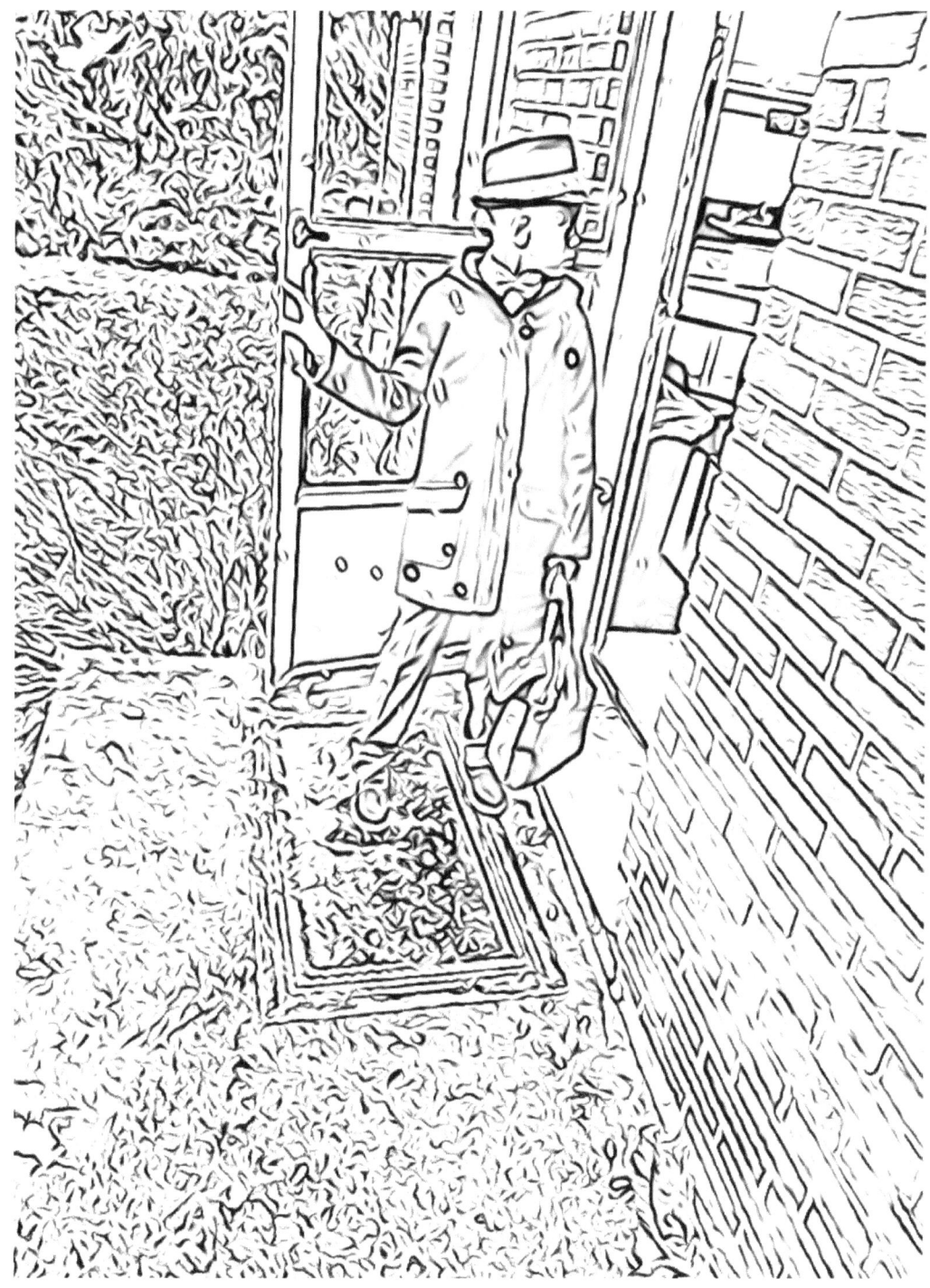

The next generation understands the power of opening doors for others because you taught your children to be considerate. Our Kindness comes from you.

Coloring With Kindness

Richard Patterson III
Kindness Comes From You

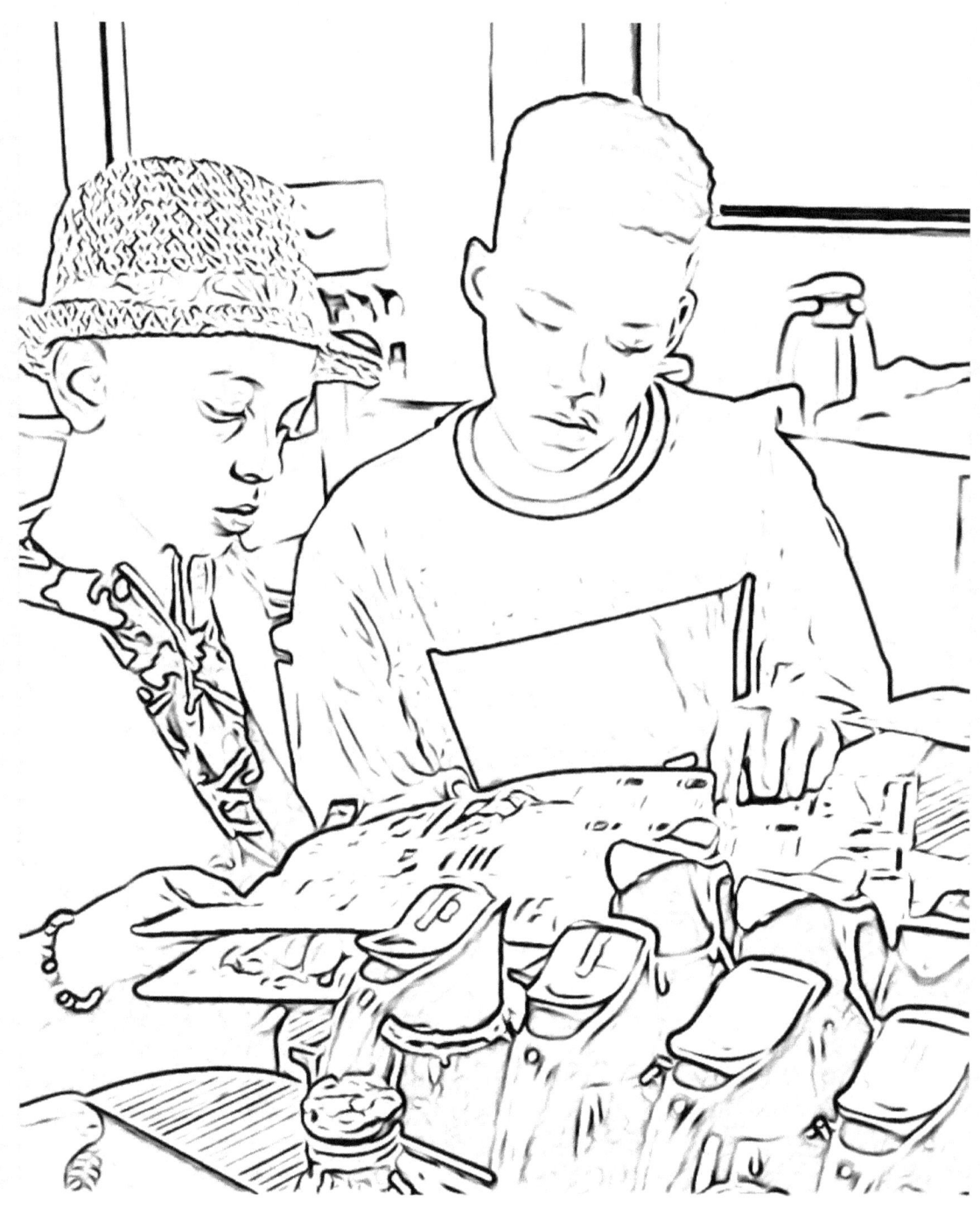

Nothing beats having a genuine interest in others. The next generation is benefiting from your Kindness.

Coloring With Kindness

Richard Patterson III
Kindness Comes From You

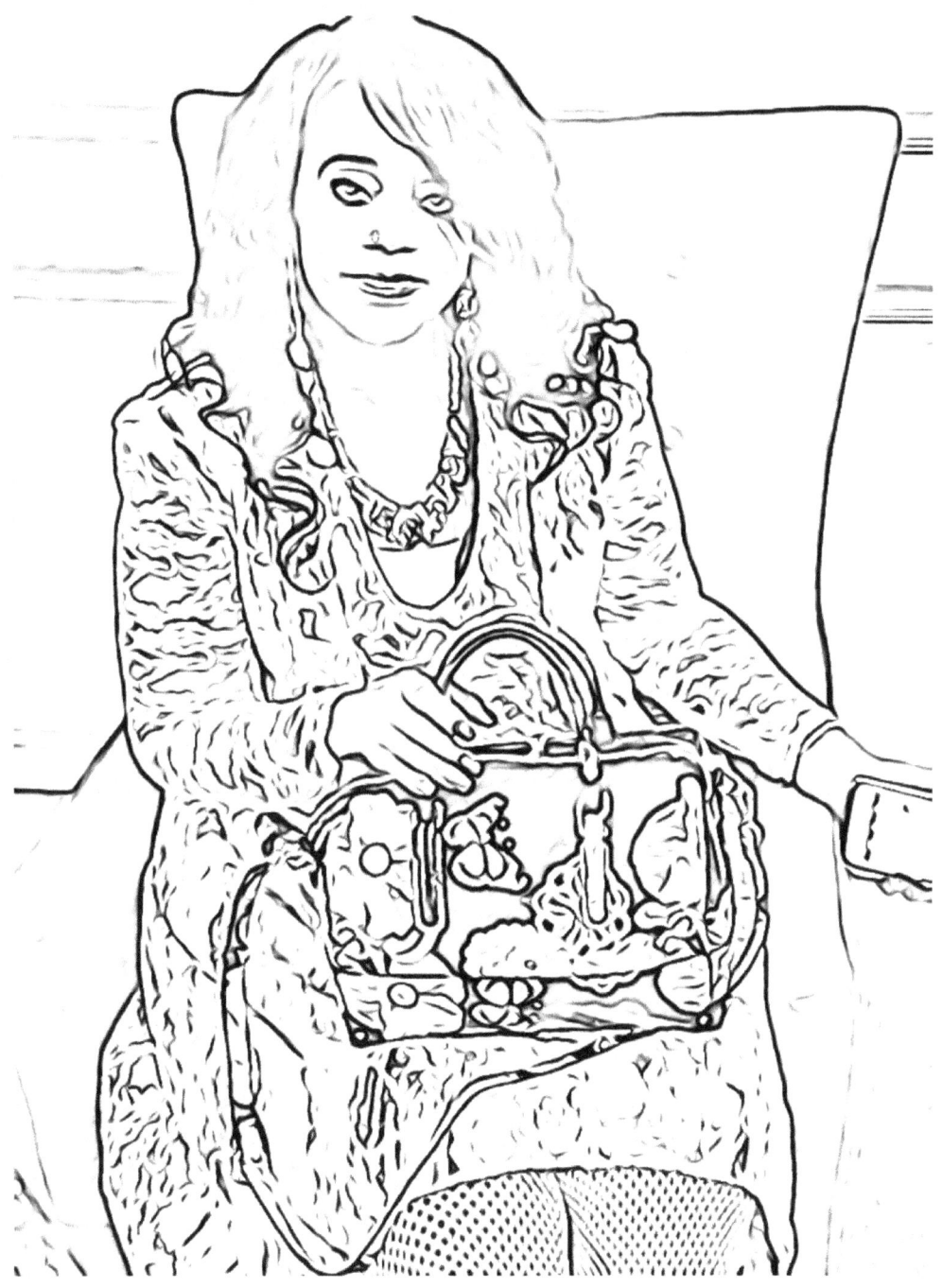

You spoke to your girls and made it clear that you have all the acceptance you need because I'm here for you. Years later your words and the time you spent is the Kindness they show to others.

Coloring With Kindness

Richard Patterson III
Kindness Comes From You

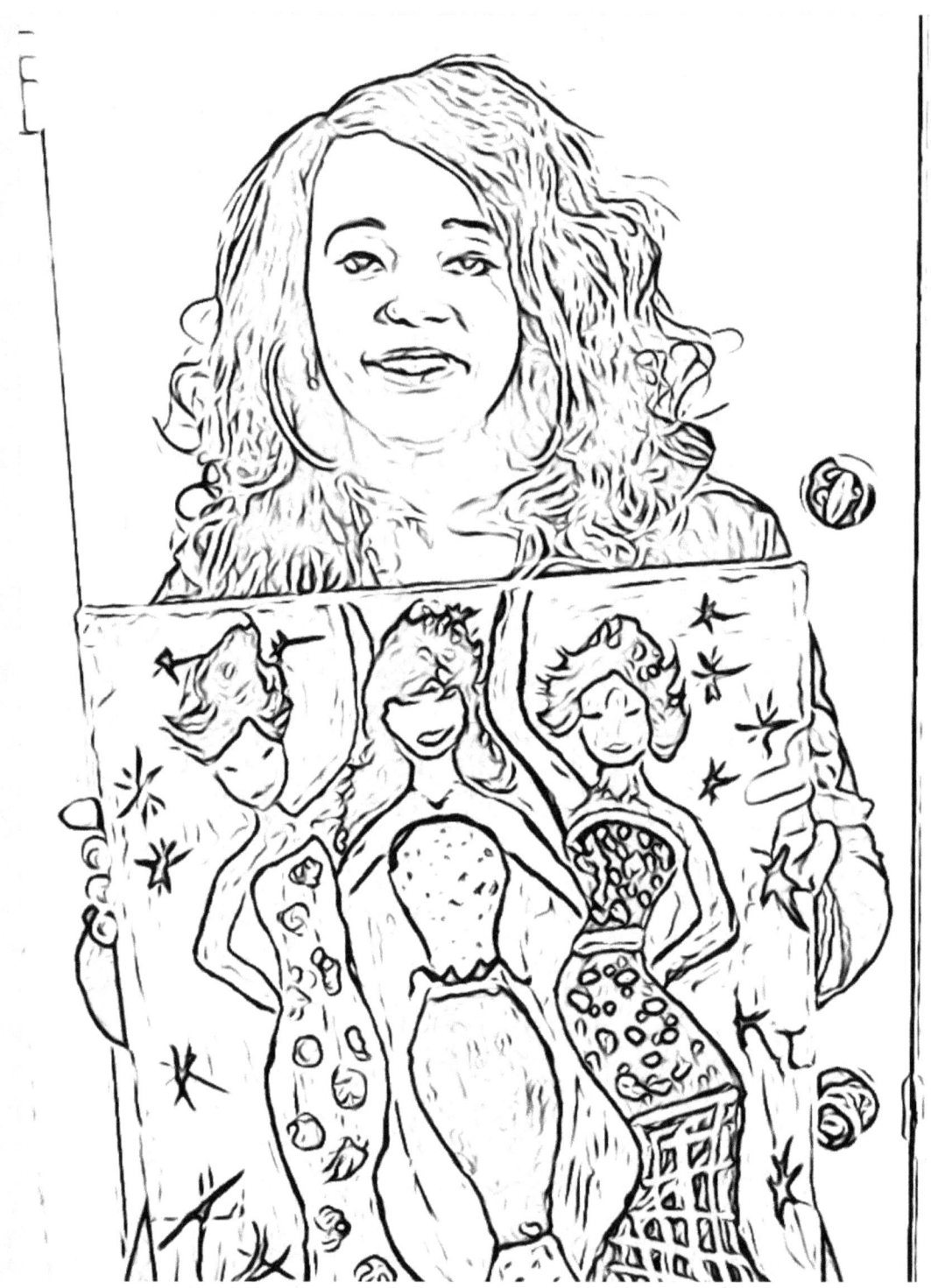

Like a painting you promoted your children to paint the colors they loved. We know who we are because of your Kindness.

Coloring With Kindness

Richard Patterson III
Kindness Comes From You

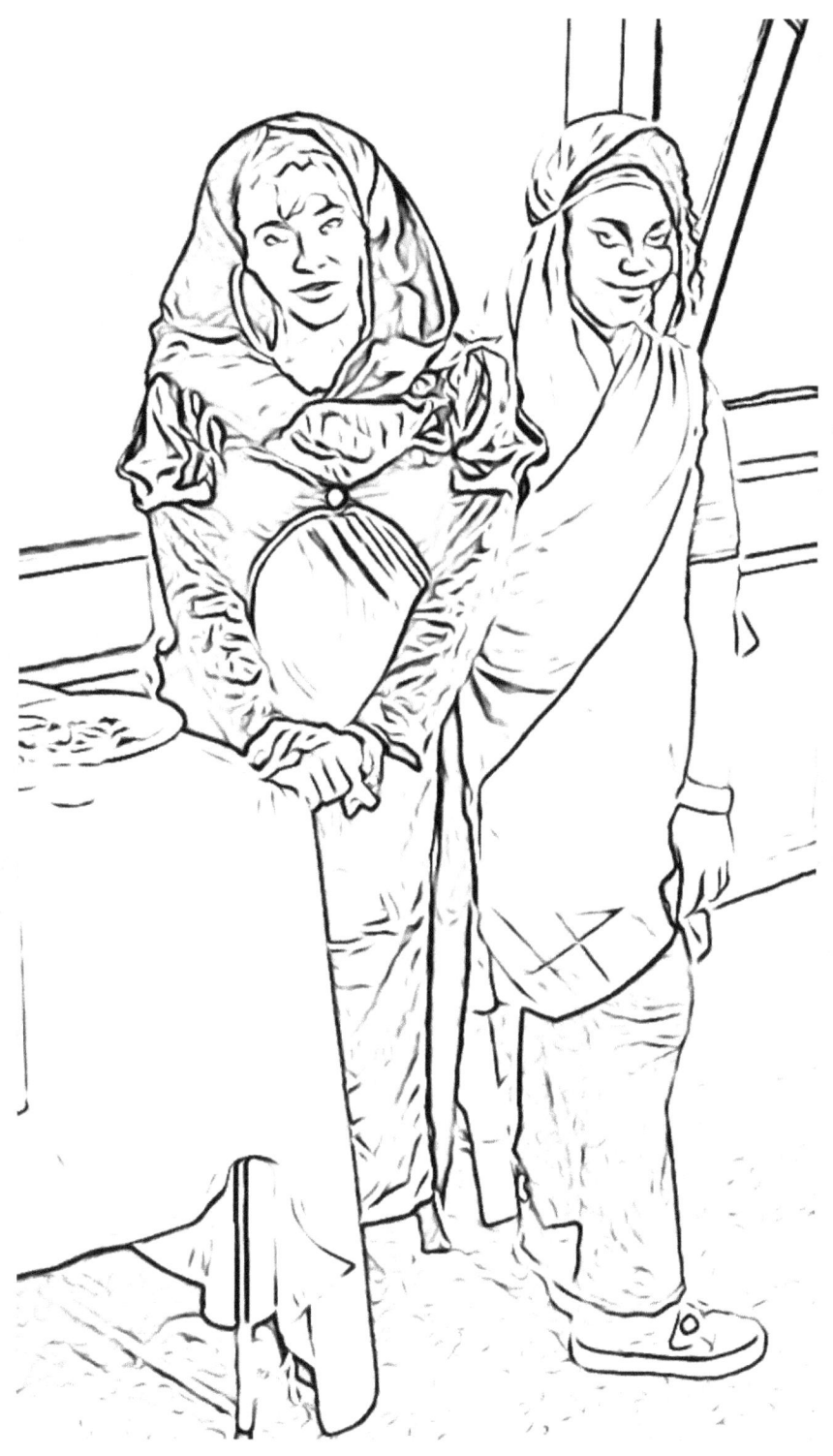

The next generation doesn't dress like you but they accept people from all walks of life. Just like you, because our Kindness comes from you.

Coloring With Kindness

Richard Patterson III
Kindness Comes From You

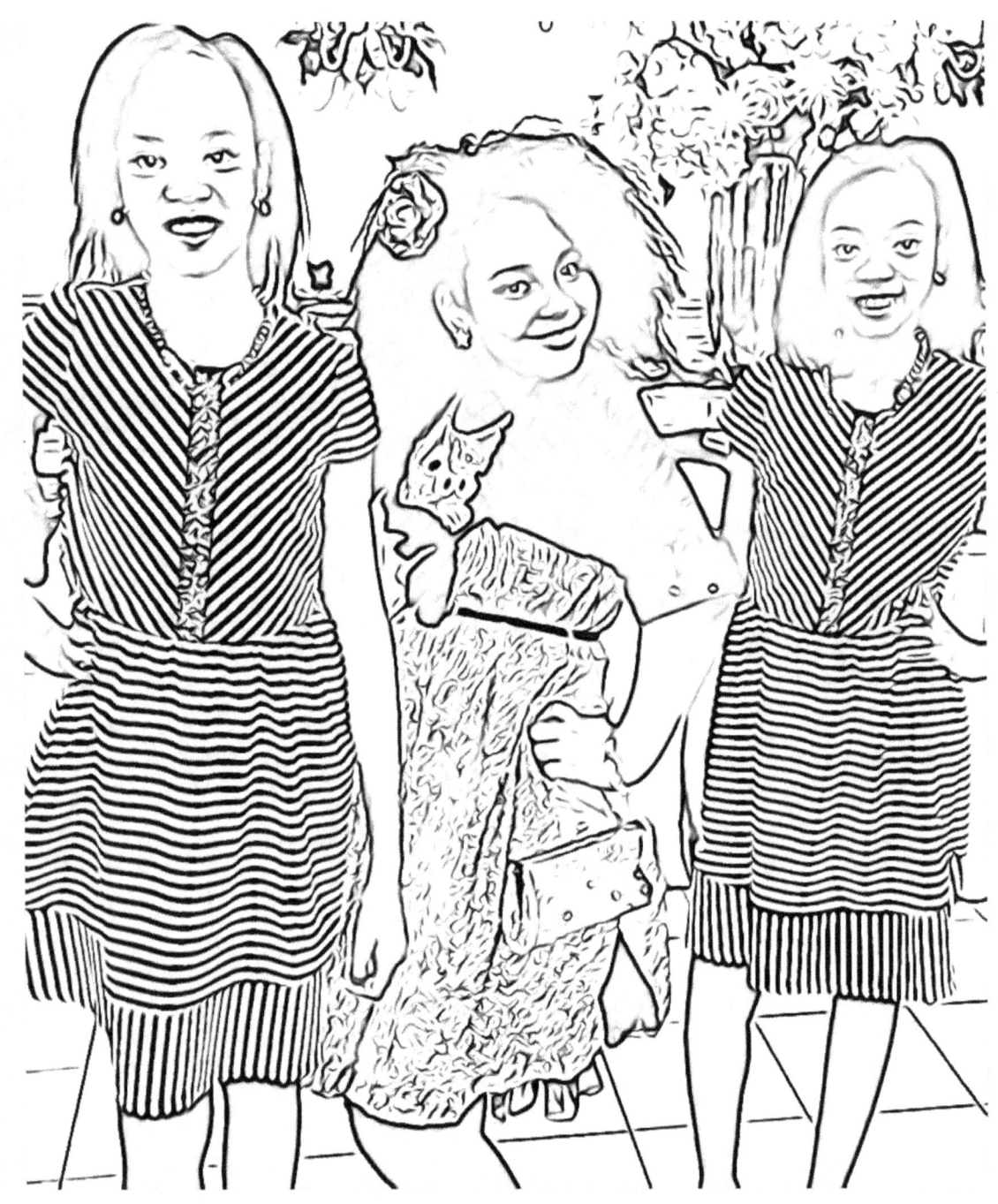

You are the personification of class and grace.
Classy and always stylish because our Kindness
comes from you.

Coloring With Kindness

Richard Patterson III
Kindness Comes From You

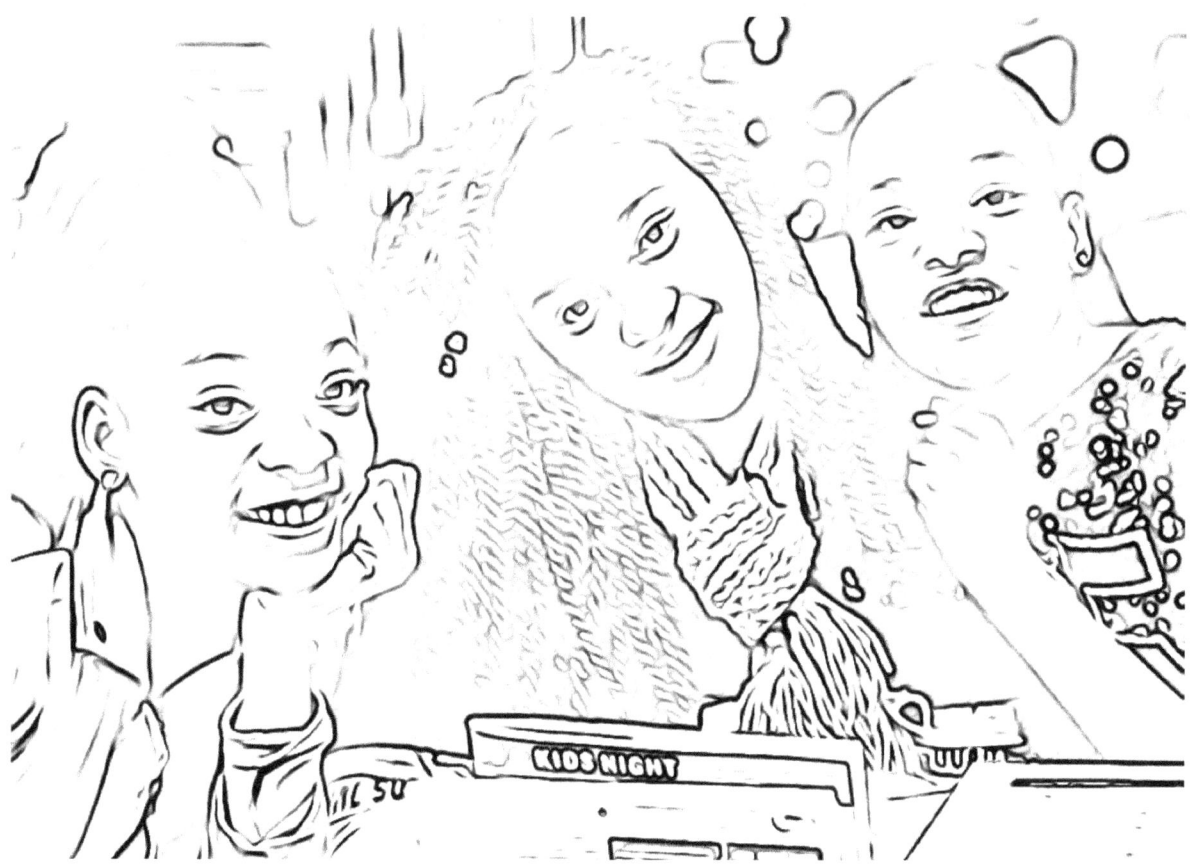

Young's girl seek to be Kind girls because you taught your daughters to always see their beauty. Now they embrace the beauty of others, because our Kindness comes from you.

Coloring With Kindness

Richard Patterson III
Kindness Comes From You

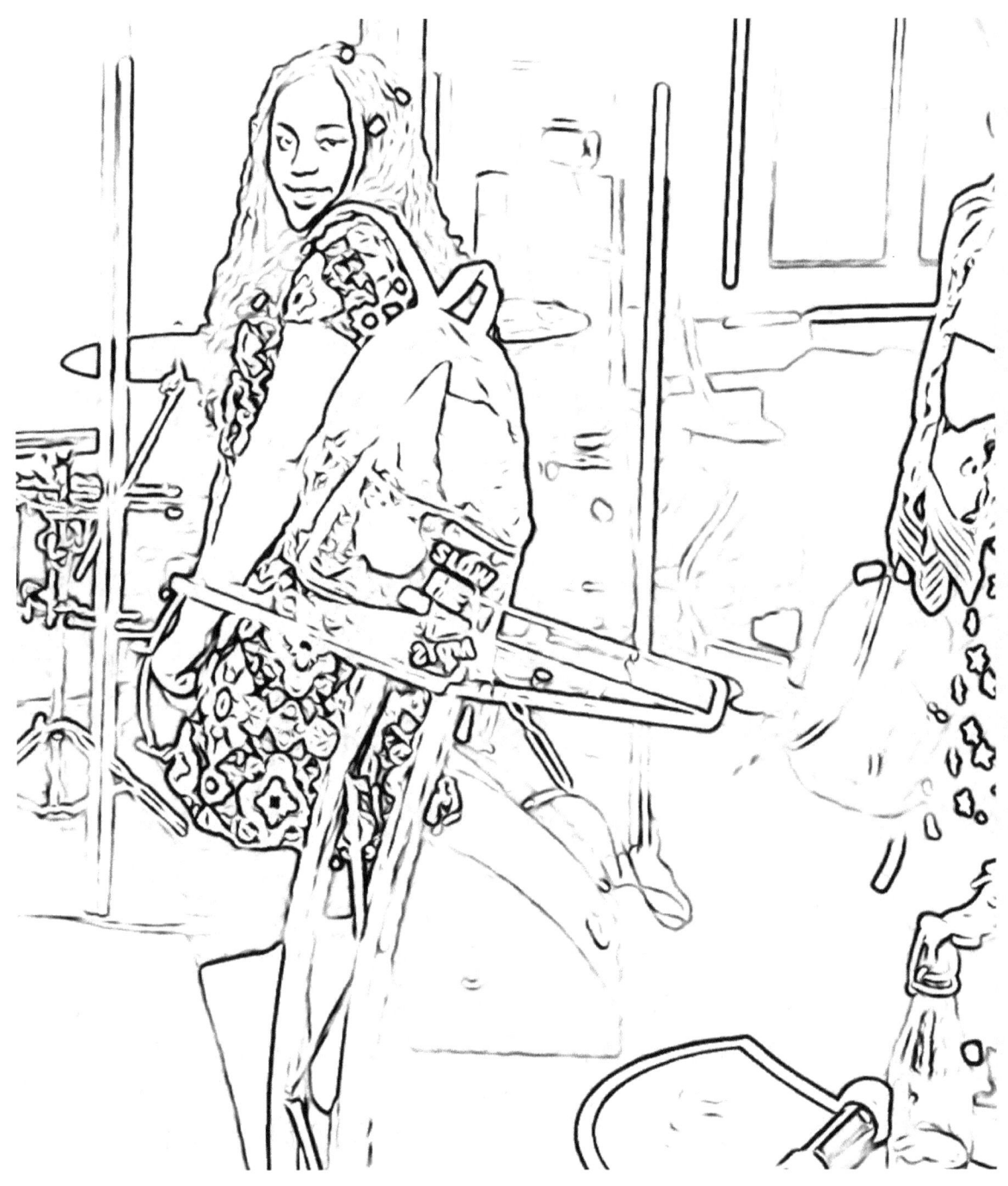

What's in your bag? You taught your children to focus on what you do have and not what you don't have. Our understanding of how to be thankful comes from you.

Coloring With Kindness

Richard Patterson III
Kindness Comes From You

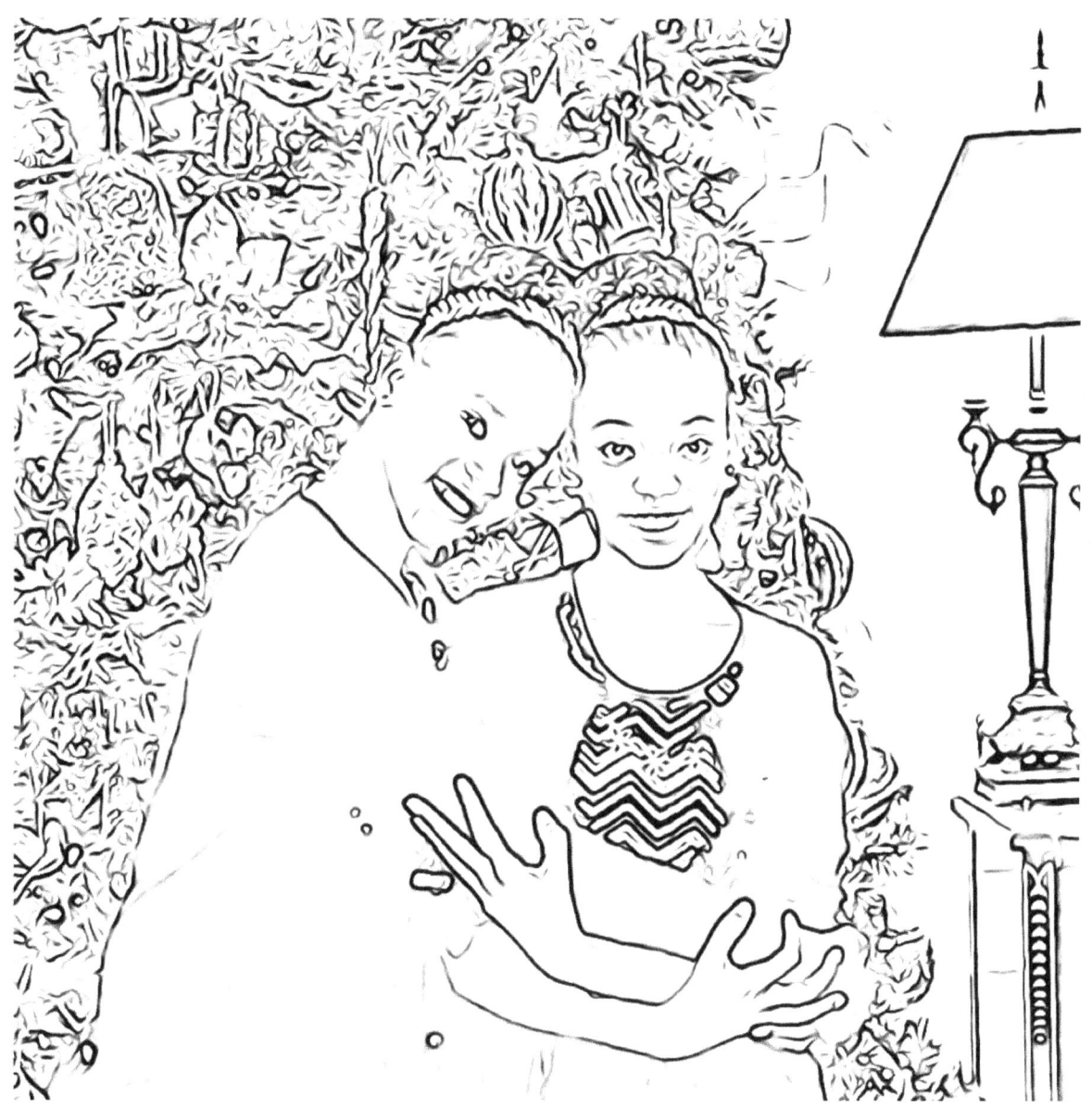

Sisterhood in this generation, is the harvest of parenthood from your generation.

Coloring With Kindness

Richard Patterson III
Kindness Comes From You

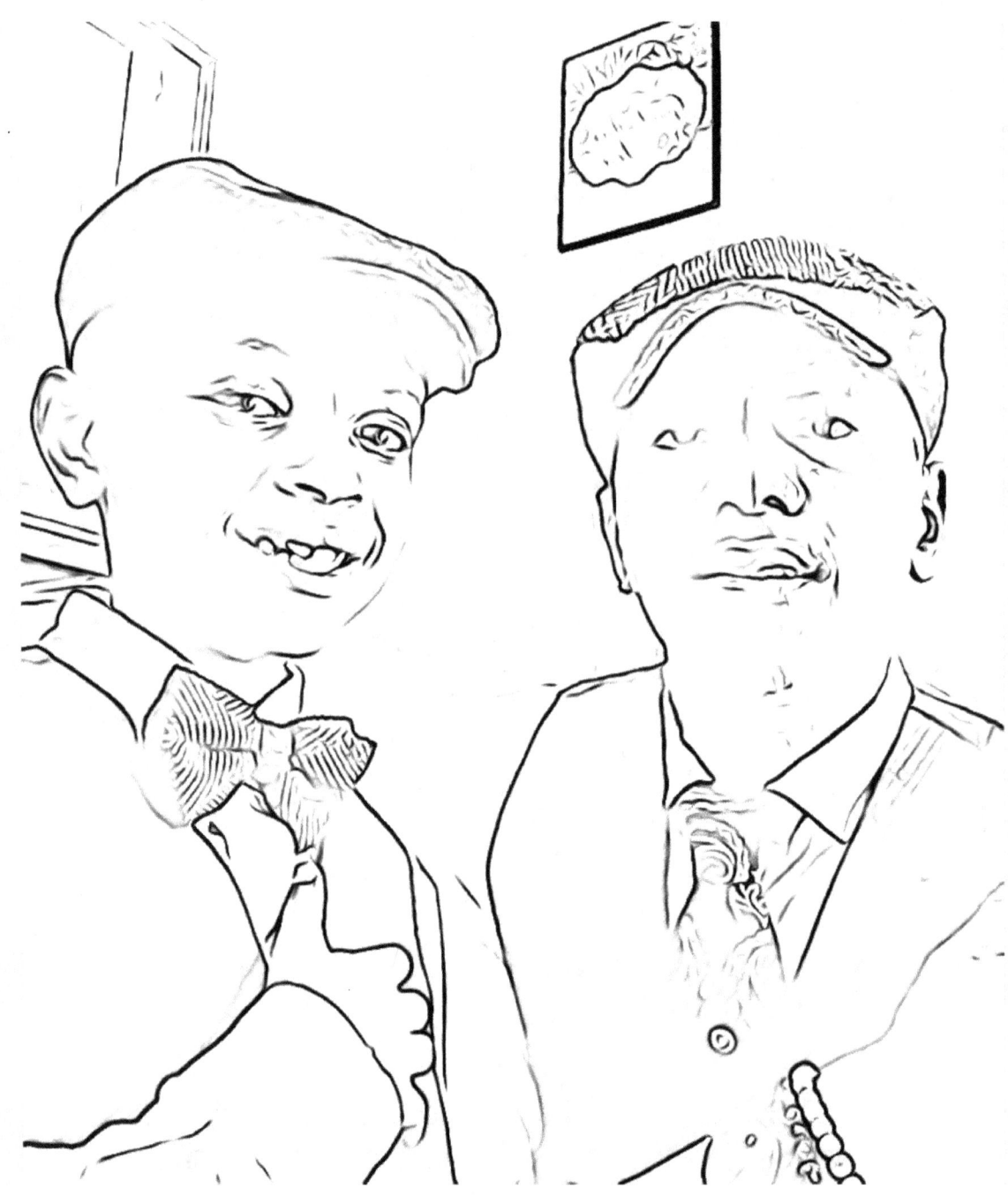

The affection that your sons express exist because our Kindness comes from you.

Coloring With Kindness

Richard Patterson III
Kindness Comes From You

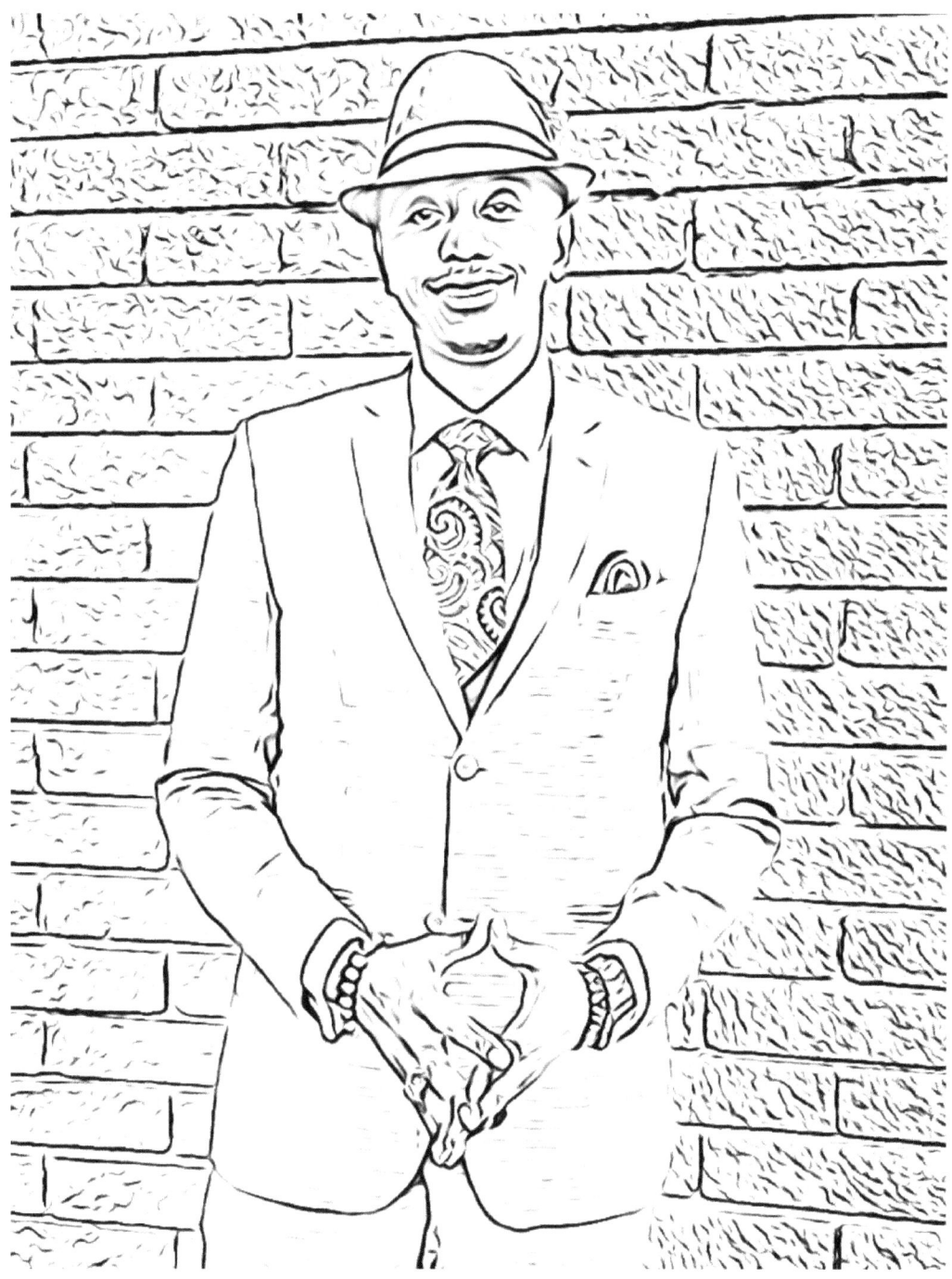

People see my drive, and ask. Where does he get it from? Everything I'm doing in ministry and in life, you showed me how to function positively without recognition. I am who I am because Kindness comes from you.

Coloring With Kindness

Richard Patterson III
Kindness Comes From You

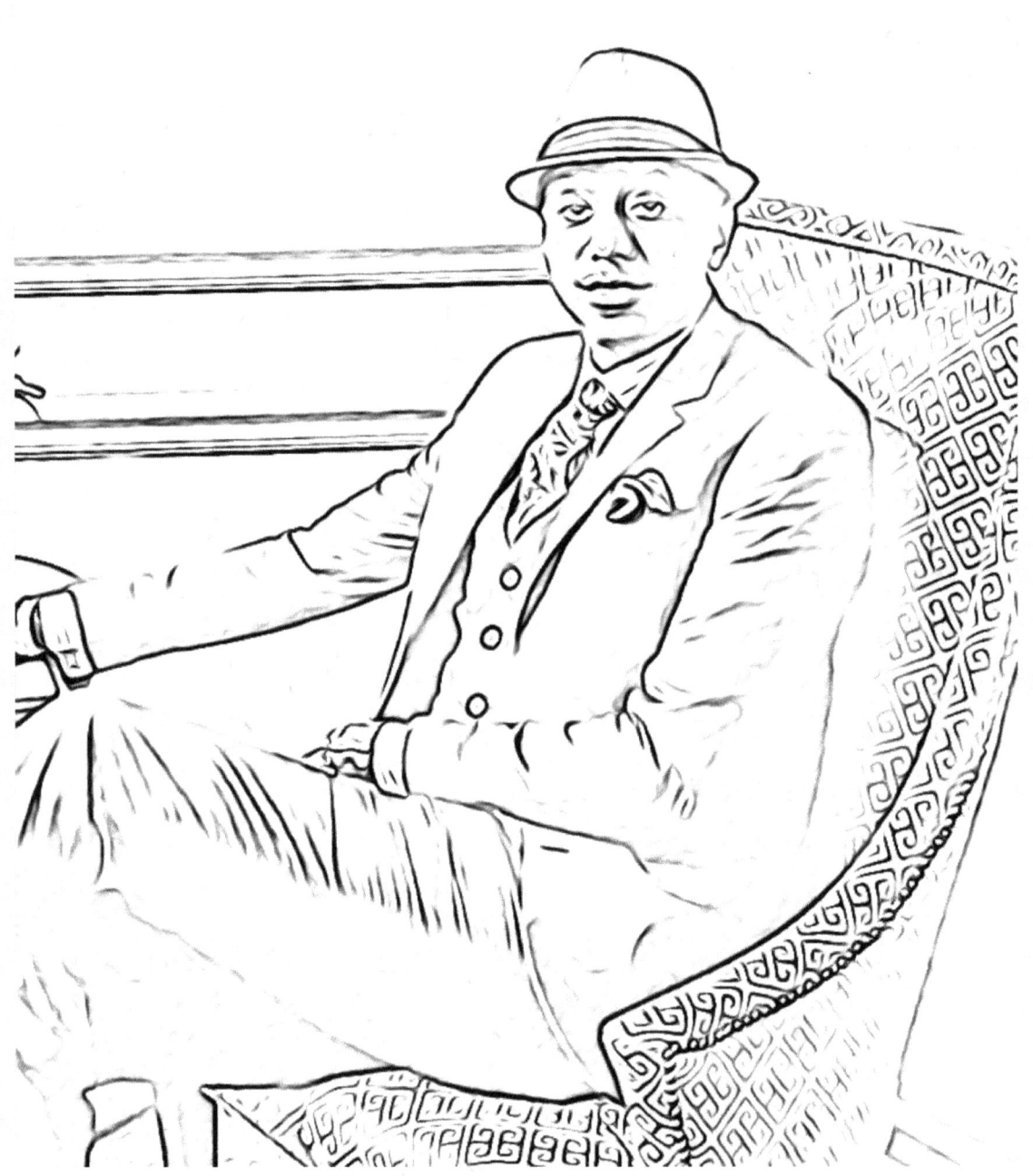

I have the confidence to be me because you spent time with me. Never discount yourself as a single mom because your son succeeds because you didn't quit.

Coloring With Kindness

Richard Patterson III
Kindness Comes From You

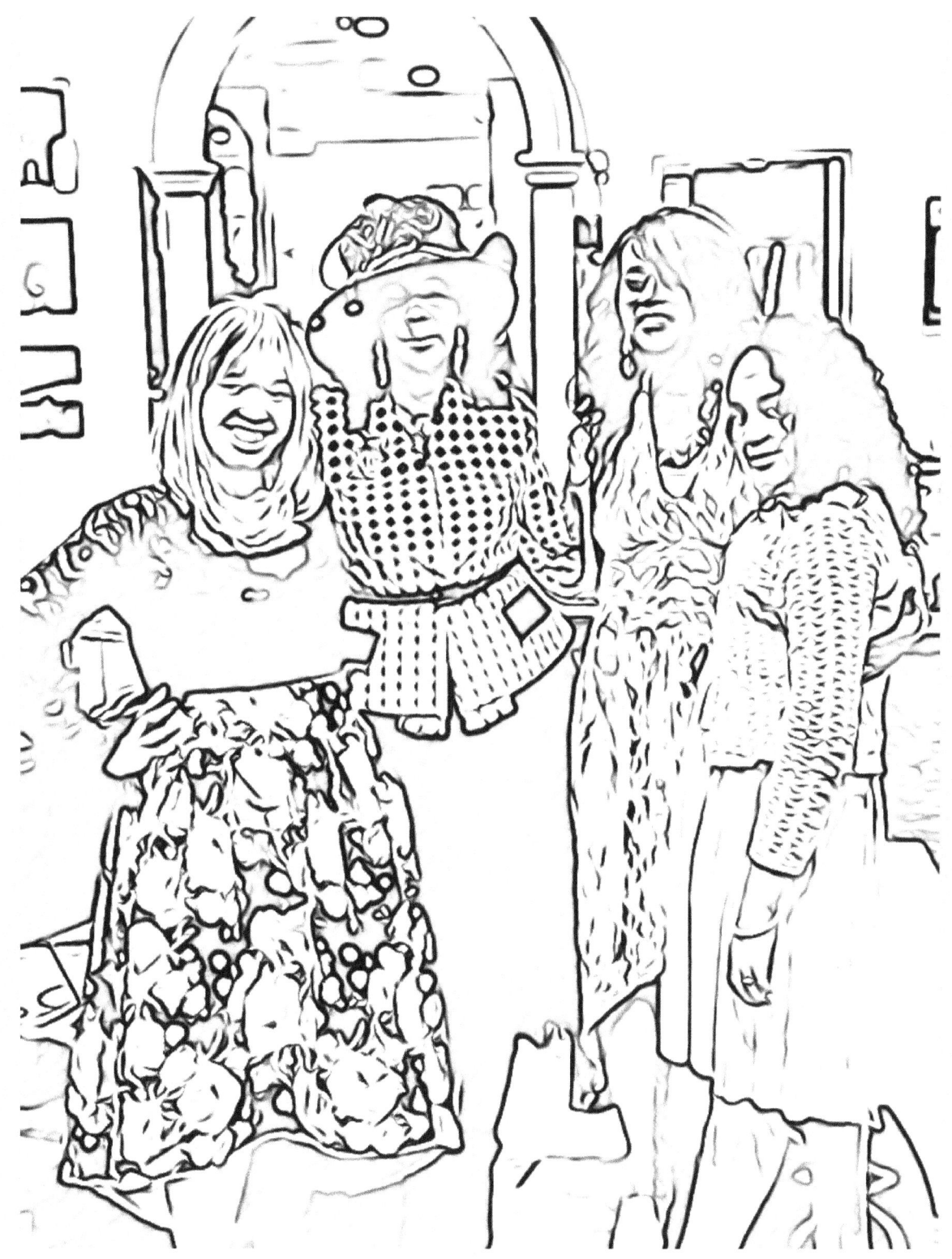

Three generations of women have a purpose and a direction in life. Because of the Kindness that comes from you.

Coloring With Kindness

Richard Patterson III
Kindness Comes From You

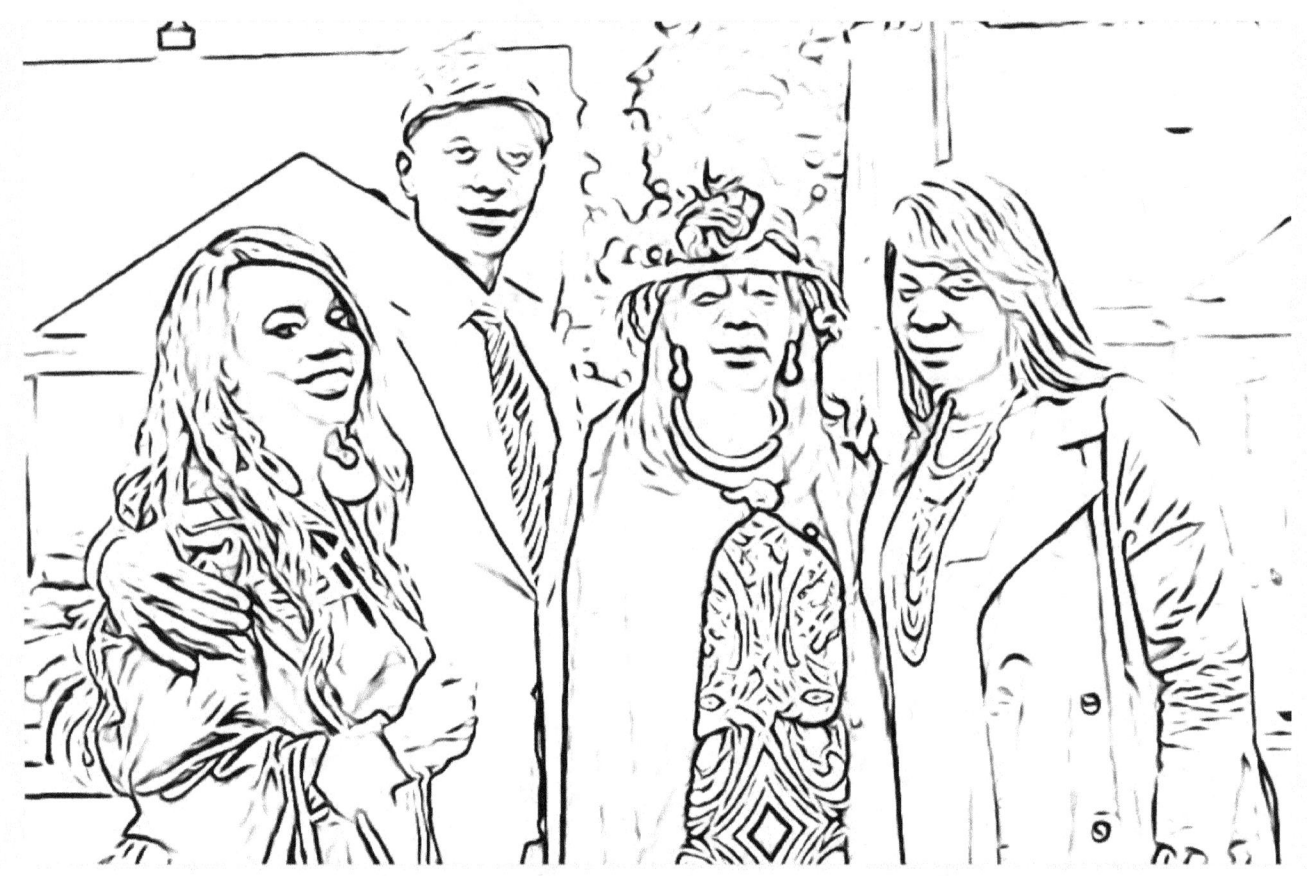

Your children call you blessed because you put your life on hold to raise them. Now we make your comfort our preference, because our Kindness comes from you.

Coloring With Kindness

Richard Patterson III
Kindness Comes From You

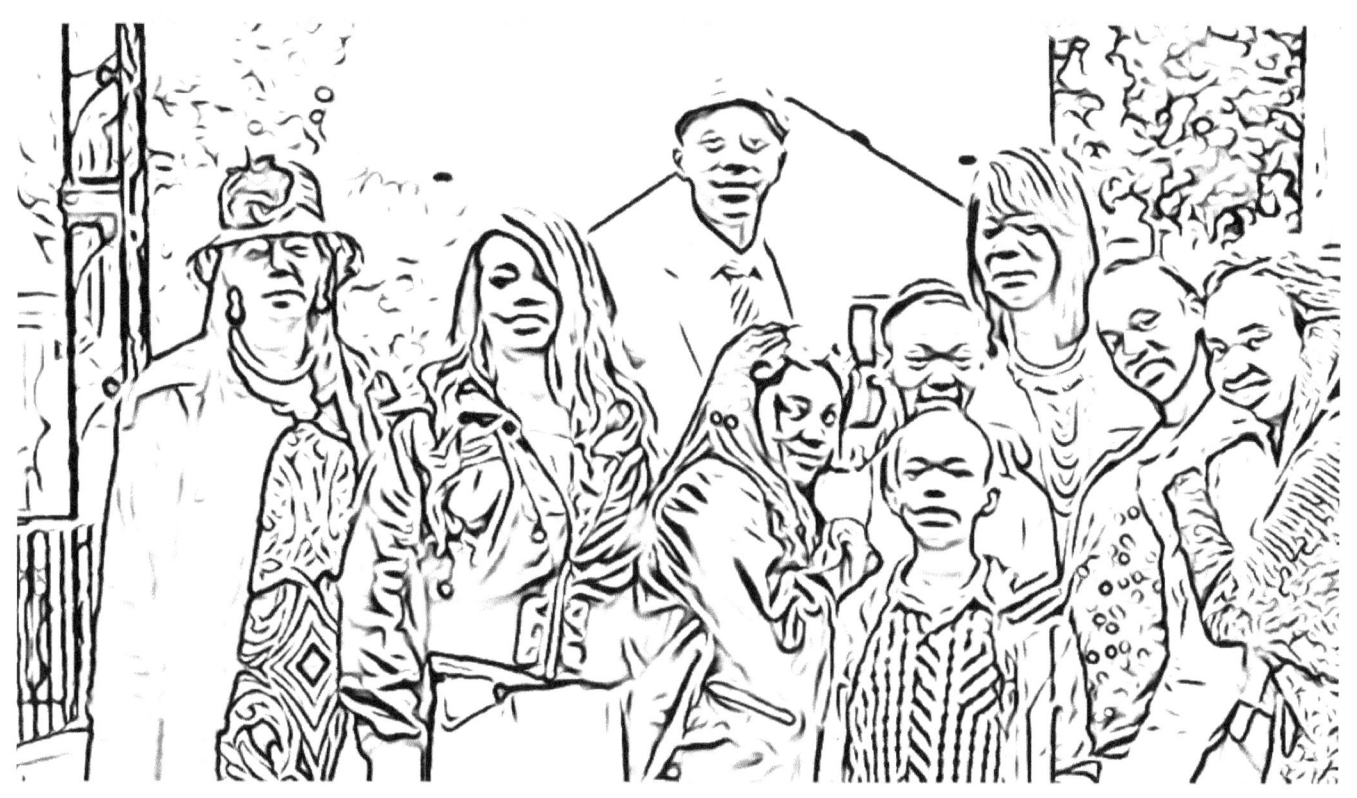

The family is strong because you are the glue that keeps us all together.

Coloring With Kindness

Richard Patterson III
Kindness Comes From You

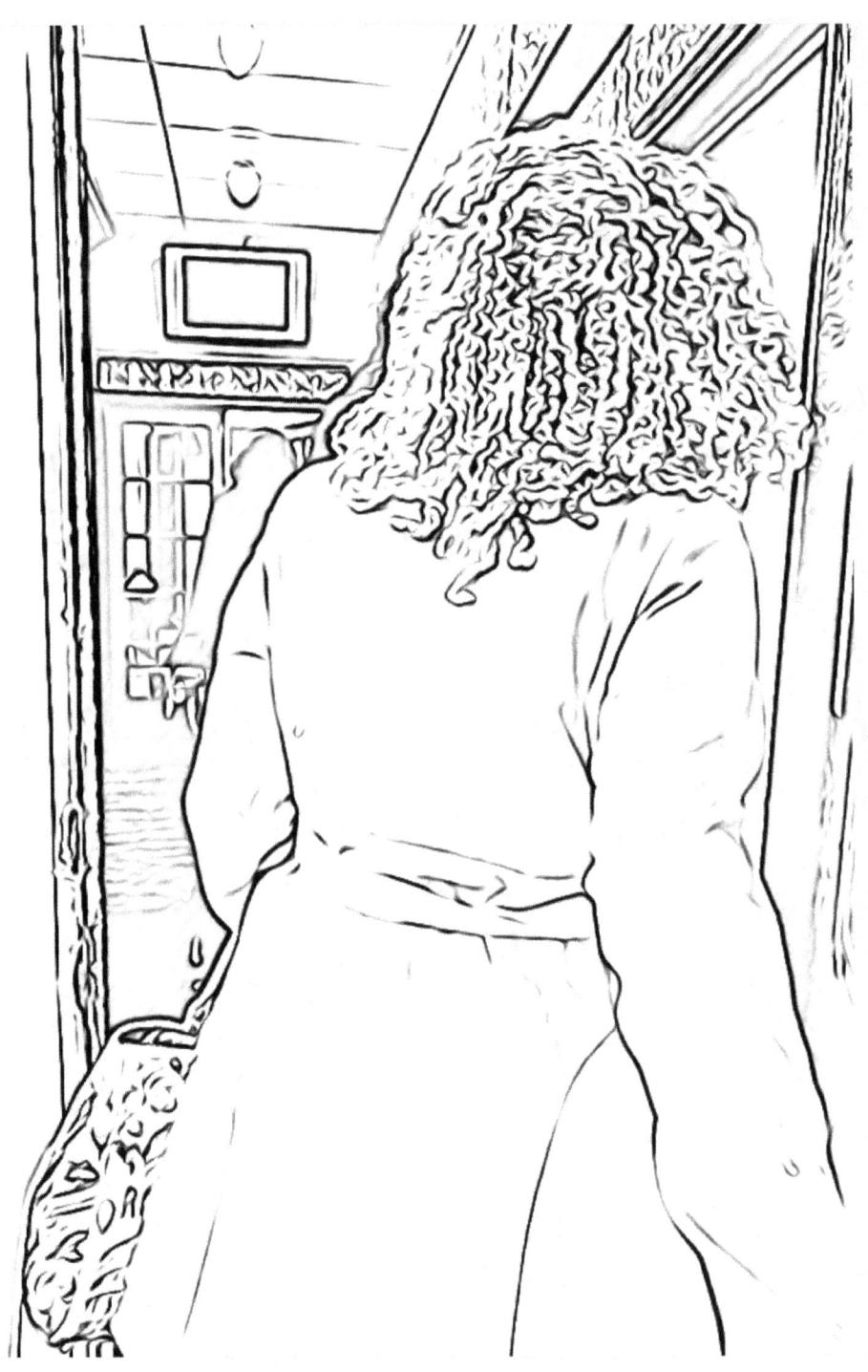

New doors don't scare us because we were taught to bring God with you no matter where you go. Keep God first is where our Kindness comes from.

Coloring With Kindness

Richard Patterson III
Kindness Comes From You

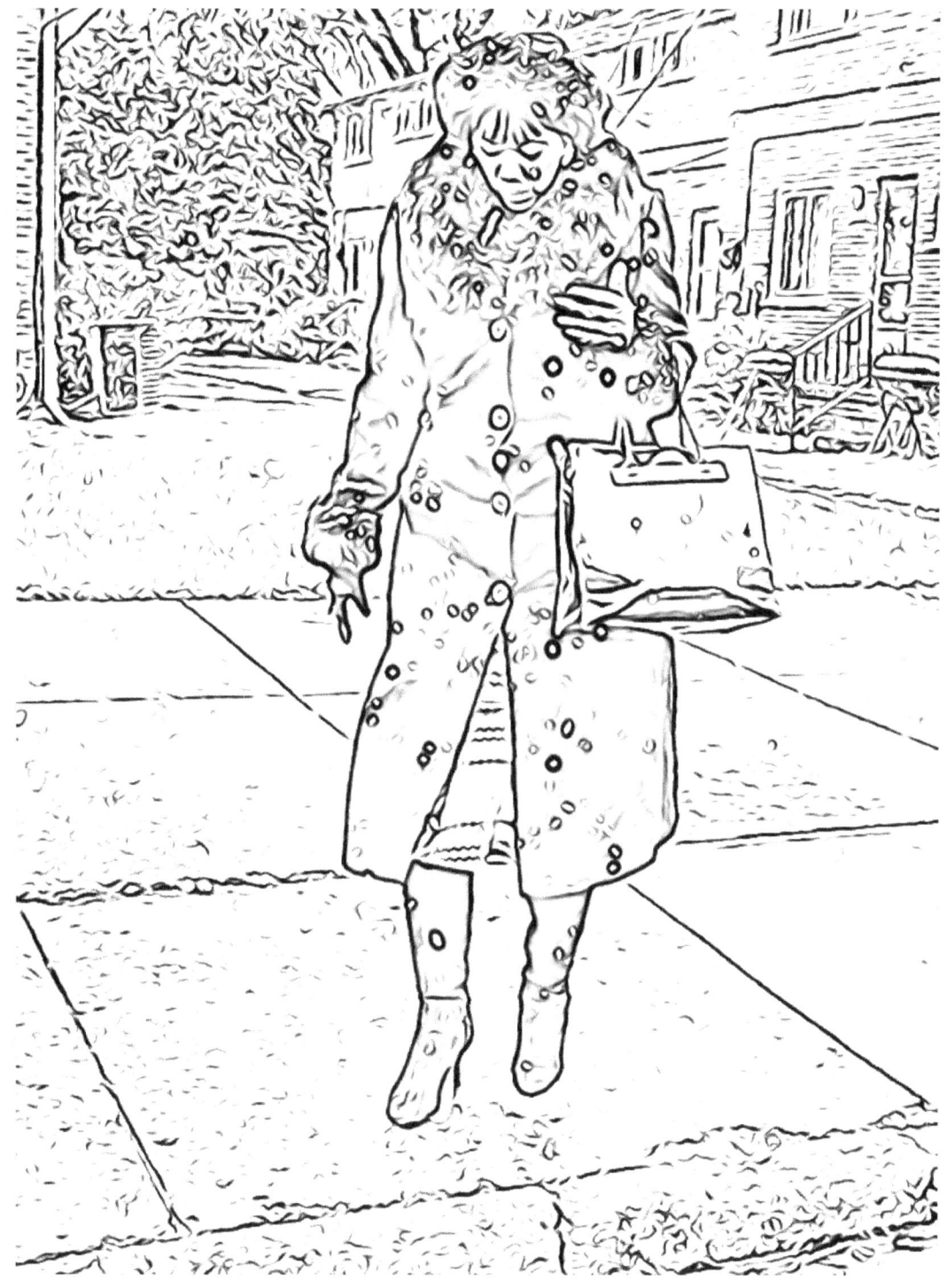

Even today your walk is a walk of faith. We see how you're trusting God and our trust in God comes from you. (The origin of our Kindness)

Coloring With Kindness

Richard Patterson III
Kindness Comes From You

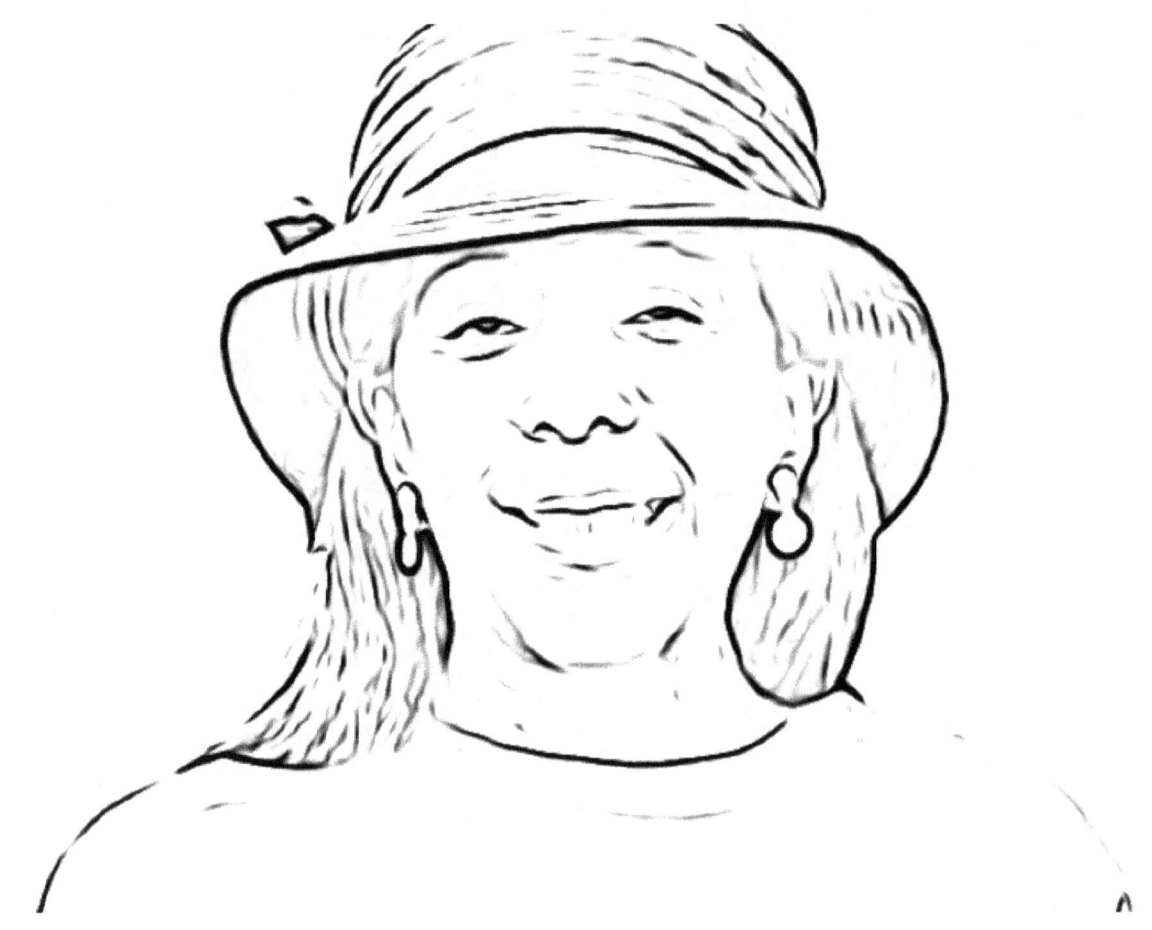

You overcame domestic abuse, raised five children and made it look easy. How did you do it? Your answer is simple "I went to God in prayer and he directed me through his Word". Having a relationship with God is where our Kindness comes from.

Coloring With Kindness

Richard Patterson III
Kindness Comes From You

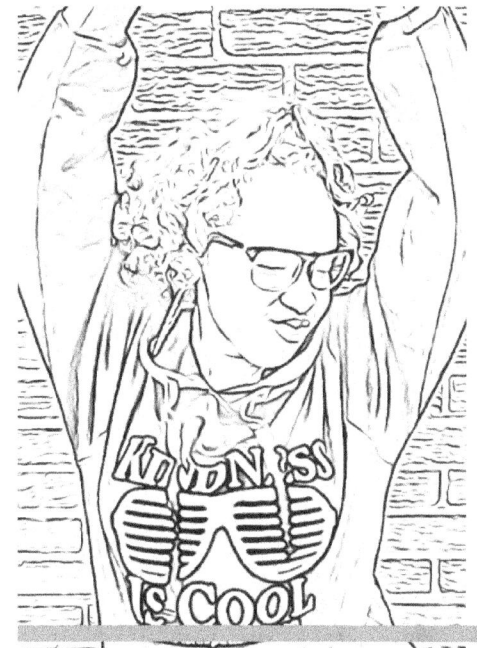

Women Celebrating other Women because Kindness Comes From You

Cultivating creativity & family values through coloring
www.richiepatterson.com

#THISISTHEKINDNESS #COLORINGWITHKINDNESS

Coloring With Kindness

Richard Patterson III
Kindness Comes From You

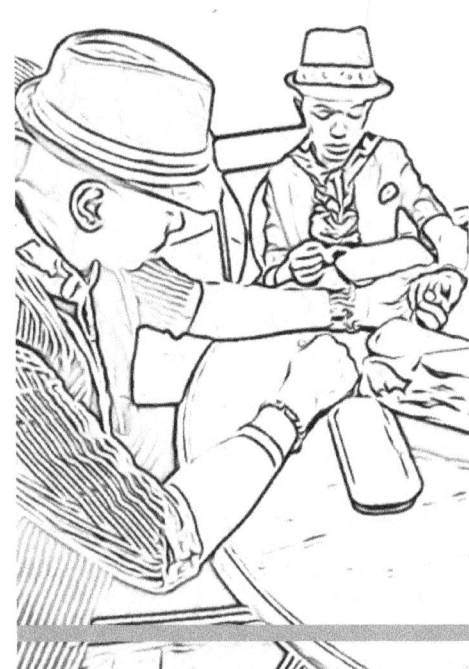

Adressing ADHD through coloring Therapist recommended

Cultivating creativity & family values through coloring
www.richiepatterson.com

#THISISTHEKINDNESS #COLORINGWITHKINDNESS

Coloring With Kindness

Richard Patterson III
Kindness Comes From You

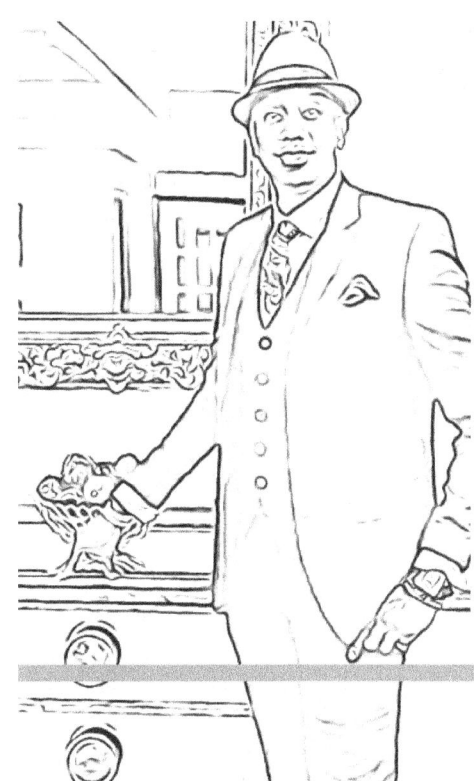

Available for Workshops, Speaking Engagements, Open Forums, Counseling Sessions And More

Pastor Richie Patterson III
8225 Allen Rd #1018
Allen Park, MI 48101
248.372.9500
www.richiepatterson.com

#THISISTHEKINDNESS
#COLORINGWITHKINDNESS

Coloring With Kindness

Richard Patterson III
Kindness Comes From You

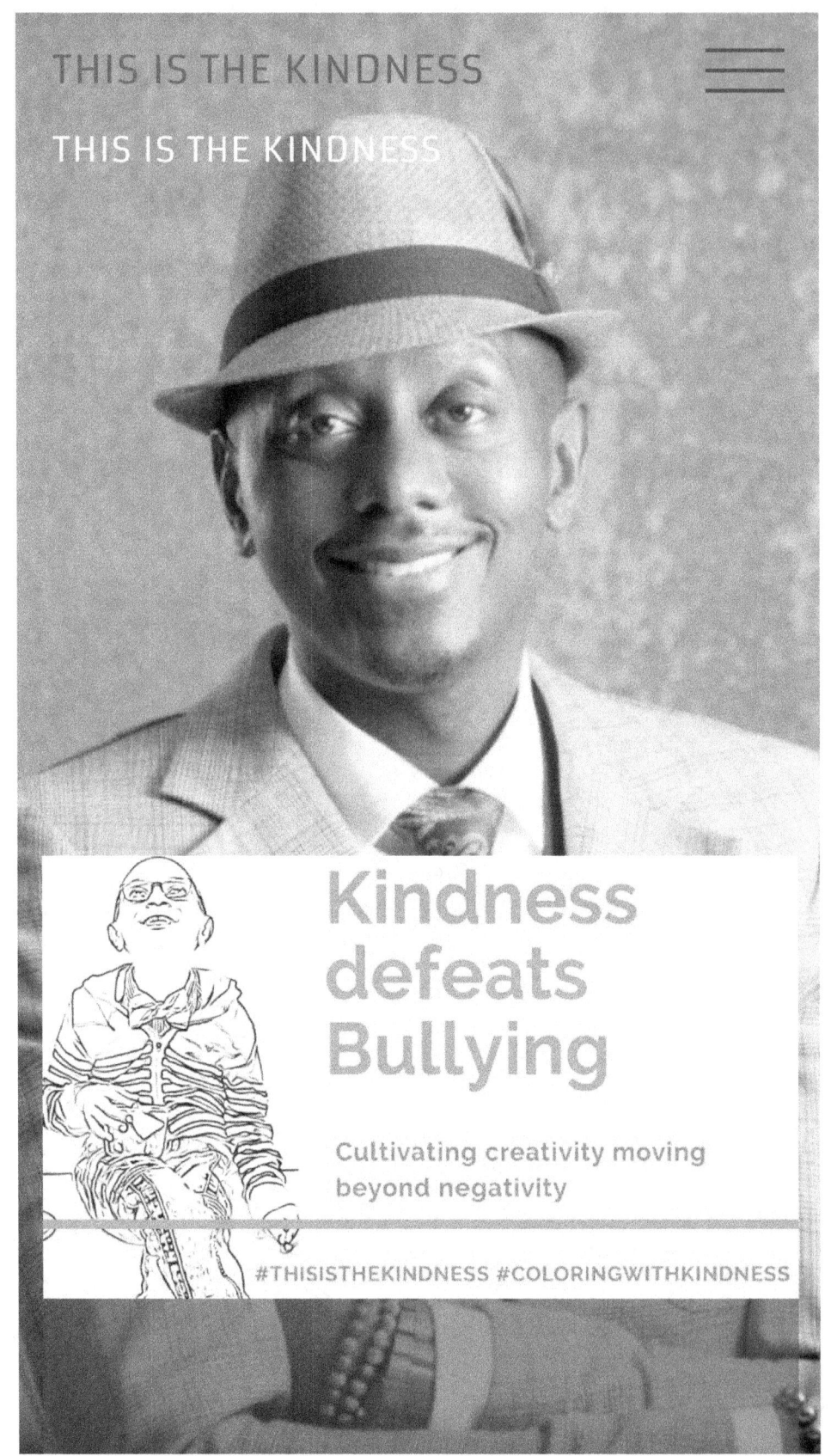

Coloring With Kindness

Richard Patterson III
Kindness Comes From You

Coloring With Kindness

Richard Patterson III
Kindness Comes From You

Coloring With Kindness

Richard Patterson III
Kindness Comes From You

Coloring With Kindness

Richard Patterson III
Kindness Comes From You

Coloring With Kindness

Richard Patterson III
Kindness Comes From You

Coloring With Kindness